Cambridge Elements

Elements in Criminology
edited by
David Weisburd
George Mason University, Virginia
Hebrew University of Jerusalem

BEYOND TRADITIONAL CONCEPTIONS OF POLICING AND CRIME CONTROL

New Metrics to Evaluate Police Performance and Improve Police Legitimacy

Dennis P. Rosenbaum
University of Illinois Chicago

CAMBRIDGE
UNIVERSITY PRESS

Shaftesbury Road, Cambridge CB2 8EA, United Kingdom

One Liberty Plaza, 20th Floor, New York, NY 10006, USA

477 Williamstown Road, Port Melbourne, VIC 3207, Australia

314–321, 3rd Floor, Plot 3, Splendor Forum, Jasola District Centre,
New Delhi – 110025, India

103 Penang Road, #05–06/07, Visioncrest Commercial, Singapore 238467

Cambridge University Press is part of Cambridge University Press & Assessment,
a department of the University of Cambridge.

We share the University's mission to contribute to society through the pursuit of
education, learning and research at the highest international levels of excellence.

www.cambridge.org
Information on this title: www.cambridge.org/9781009612760

DOI: 10.1017/9781009612784

When citing this work, please include a reference to the DOI 10.1017/9781009612784

First published 2025

A catalogue record for this publication is available from the British Library

ISBN 978-1-009-61276-0 Hardback
ISBN 978-1-009-61279-1 Paperback
ISSN 2633-3341 (online)
ISSN 2633-3333 (print)

Additional resources for this publication at www.cambridge.org/Rosenbaum

Beyond Traditional Conceptions of Policing and Crime Control

New Metrics to Evaluate Police Performance and Improve Police Legitimacy

Elements in Criminology

DOI: 10.1017/9781009612784
First published online: June 2025

Dennis P. Rosenbaum
University of Illinois Chicago

Author for correspondence: Dennis P. Rosenbaum,
dennisrosenbaum3@gmail.com

Abstract: Today, policing in the United States is facing a crisis of legitimacy and calls for reform. This Element examines this crisis and describes the adverse effects of problematic police behavior on community members, police officers, and public safety. A critical analysis of past reform efforts is offered, including why they have had limited success in changing police operations, police culture, or styles of policing. The central thesis of this Element is that most police reforms have failed because we continue to use the wrong metrics to evaluate police performance. Cities have yet to systematically measure what matters to the public, namely, how people are treated by the police. Hence, the Element proposes a new system of accountability using data from body-worn cameras (BWCs) and contact surveys to measure and incentivize procedural justice. Translating evidence into real organizational change should improve street-level policing, enhance police legitimacy, and improve public safety.

Keywords: police, legitimacy, accountability, procedural justice, reform

ISBNs: 9781009612760 (HB), 9781009612791 (PB), 9781009612784 (OC)
ISSNs: 2633-3341 (online), 2633-3333 (print)

Contents

1 Introduction

History is replete with efforts to reform American policing, yet this institution continues to suffer from a "crisis of legitimacy." This Element begins by defining police legitimacy and the various ways that legitimacy has been jeopardized by police practices. The costs associated with the current model of policing are summarized, including the adverse impact on community members, police officers, and public safety. Some constitutionally protected populations are particularly vulnerable to police mistreatment, including people of color, the LGBTQ+ community, persons with mental illness, victims of crime, the homeless, and youth.

This review is followed by an analysis of reform efforts and why they have been ineffective in changing street-level policing and increasing public trust in the police. Weak implementation has contributed to this failure, but the primary barrier to success has been the overreliance on enforcement statistics to evaluate police performance. When evaluating the police, our society needs to "measure what matters" to the public, namely, how they are treated by the police. Giving voice to service recipients is critical for improving service and reducing any biases in treatment.

Hence, this Element offers a new, evidence-based approach to police innovation that should yield significant changes in police culture and improvements in police-community relations. New systems of measurement are described that focus on procedural justice and effective communication skills during police-public encounters. These reforms will require the routine collection, analysis, and utilization of data, along with advanced data analytics and artificial intelligence, to assess differences in policing across different types of calls for service, geographic areas, police units, supervisors, individual officers, and community members. Thus, new approaches to analyzing new datasets are proposed to advance our knowledge of policing and our understanding of police-public encounters. Bringing together two camps in criminology, this framework offers a clear link between process and outcome metrics, between officers' treatment of the public and public safety.

Policing scholars have been outstanding in measuring specific constructs, like procedural justice, but the collection of good data will have absolutely no impact on police behavior or police legitimacy unless they are applied to police organizational practices. Translational criminology requires that we translate evidence into practice. Hence, this Element proposes evidence-based organizational changes that use new data to incentivize "good policing."

Finally, this Element proposes "big science" to test the feasibility of this model prior to full-scale implementation. A proof-of-concept demonstration, with rigorous evaluations in multiple cities, will provide a road map for institutionalizing a national system of performance measurement and accountability. This level of innovation, with strong implementation fidelity, should increase procedural justice, increase police legitimacy, strengthen police-community relations, and increase public safety throughout the United States.

2 Police Legitimacy

Over a century ago, Max Weber conceived of legitimacy as something that people with power and authority must earn from those who are expected to follow them (Waeraas, 2009). In the policing field, legitimacy is judged, to a large extent, by whether the public believes that the police will act in the best interest of the community and whether they feel obligated to obey legal authorities (Tyler, 2006, 2014; Tyler & Jackson, 2013). Thus, police authority is not defined entirely by the badge, gun, or their legal powers but is also based on the public's perception of them and is authorized by the "consent of the governed." Police legitimacy is defined by the hearts and minds of the public.

Along these lines, the President's Task Force on 21st Century Policing (2015) opened its report by underscoring the importance of public trust: "Trust between law enforcement agencies and the people they protect and serve is essential in a democracy. It is key to the stability of our communities, the integrity of our criminal justice system, and the safe and effective delivery of police services" (p. 1).

3 The Cost of Modern Policing

Emerging from the southern slave patrols in 1704 (Dulaney, 2015; Reichel, 2022), American policing has an ugly history of brutality and political corruption that repeatedly undermined the legitimacy of the institution. Officers who worked for city police in the nineteenth century had unlimited authority to administer "street justice" and were part of a corrupt system of government (Walker, 1977). After the civil war, the police were called upon to enforced "Jim Crow" laws for nearly 100 years. As a result, police brutality, deviance, and racial bias have been the subject of critical analysis for more than a century (Johnson, 2003; Kappeler et al., 1998; Nelson, 2000).

Essentially, American policing failed to follow some of the basic principles of modern policing as articulated by Sir Robert Peel when the London Metropolitan Police Force was created in 1829. In terms of legitimacy, the Peelian principles emphasized the importance of "policing by consent" and gaining the public's respect by minimizing use of force and arrests and maximizing crime prevention. That has not happened. Consequently, we have seen a rapid growth in publications that criticize police militarization and police violence, such as *Rise of the Warrior Cop* (Balko, 2014), *Our Enemies in Blue* (Williams, 2015), *Police State* (Spence, 2015), and many others. Public dissatisfaction with police performance has also resulted in calls to "defund" and even "abolish" the police among social justice advocates (Purnell, 2021).

The costs of police misconduct and biased enforcement against vulnerable members have been significant, including the adverse effects of investigatory stops, use of force, arrests, and general mistreatment of the public. This has resulted in anti-police movements, as well as negative effects on public safety, officer safety, and taxpayers.

To deter future crime, we want the police to enforce the law, but as Lum and Nagin (2017, p. 344) point out, "arrests are costly to all involved – the police who make them, the public who must pay for the ensuing punishment, and the individual who must endure that punishment." Local and county law enforcement cost taxpayers roughly $100 billion per year (Buehler, 2021). However, that figure does not include the cost of human life or police misconduct lawsuits. In the United States, there are more than 1,000 fatal police shootings each year (*Washington Post*, 2024), and lawsuits cost taxpayers billions of dollars in misconduct settlements (Alexander et al., 2022).

Aggressive policing and misconduct are not only financially expensive – they are also costly in terms of police legitimacy and public safety. As discussed in this Element, when the public does not view the police as legitimate authority figures who "do the right thing," a number of adverse consequences occur, and these effects can undermine public safety.

3.1 Bias Against Vulnerable Groups

I am most concerned about the unconstitutional treatment of the vulnerable classes. The 14th Amendment of the US Constitution guarantees "due process" and "equal protection" of the law for all groups, including those defined by race, color, sex, gender identity, age, religion, mental health, disability, national origin, sexual orientation, and other at-risk groups. Clearly, not all Americans are treated equally by the police. Today, police critics are insisting on fairer and more respectful treatment of vulnerable, constitutionally protected classes. Mistreatment has been highlighted recently in our national dialogue, so we must understand better how these vulnerable groups are being treated and what can be done to improve the police services they receive.

The history of racism in American is well documented in classic works such as *The Souls of Black Folk* (Du Bois, 1903), *The Nature of Prejudice* (Allport, 1954), and *The Warmth of Other Suns* (Wilkerson, 2011). Racial bias during enforcement is nothing new and is also well documented. The National

Advisory Commission on Civil Disorder (1968) – called the Kerner Commission – attributed the national race riots of 1967 to white racism and blamed police mistreatment of Black Americans as the spark that started the riots. The Commission recommended that agencies "[r]eview police operations in the ghetto to ensure proper conduct by police officers, and eliminate abrasive practices" (p. 8). In the context of racial inequality and poverty and growing frustration and anger over discrimination, white officers making arrests and engaging in brutality against Black community members was enough to trigger numerous protests and riots (Evans, 2021). The reports from multiple commissions, beginning with the 1919 Chicago riots, all reached a similar conclusion.

The problem of racial discrimination by the police has continued in recent decades. Racial profiling and violations of civil liberties during the drug war in the 1980s and 1990s contributed significantly to the problem of disproportionate arrest and incarceration of Black community members (Rosenbaum, 1993). The incidents of extreme police violence against Black people that have resulted in protests over the past sixty years do not capture the widespread nature of the problem today. National data collected through the Police-Public Contact Survey have consistently revealed that Blacks and Hispanics are more likely than whites to experience either the threat of force or actual force during their contact with the police, more likely to receive enforcement actions, and more likely to feel that the officer engaged in misconduct, such as slurs, bias, or sexual misbehavior (Harrell & Davis, 2020; Tapp & Davis, 2022).

A meta-analysis of twenty-seven separate datasets shows clearly that suspects of color have been arrested at higher rates than white suspects (Kochel et al., 2011). Furthermore, Black and Hispanic community members are shot and killed by the police at a much higher rate than white community members (Washington Post, 2024). Even when guns are not used, an analysis of 1,000 deaths shows that Black persons, who comprise 12 percent of the US population, represented one-third of all deaths involving physical force by the police across many cities (Dunklin et al., 2024).

Some have argued that the racial disparities in enforcement are largely the result of the concentration of crime in low-income neighborhoods where people of color are overrepresented rather than expressions of racial prejudice by the police (Engel & Swartz, 2014). Taking a longitudinal look at the criminal histories of roughly 1,000 youth over time, Sampson and Neil (2024) conclude that persistent racial disparities in arrest rates can be attributed to "concentrated and cumulative forms of neighborhood disadvantages and advantages that are spatially concentrated" (p. 198). Clearly, higher crime rates in underresourced communities has resulted in more concentrated policing and arrests, regardless of whether the arrestees have a history of criminality or the police are expressing racial bias. However, for this

Element, my point is that the methods of aggressive policing are real and enforcement is problematic regardless of the cause.

There are long-term consequences of enforcement. In addition to death or injury, police enforcement over time has resulted in the mass incarceration of Black people (Alexander, 2011). Critics have also argued that the criminal justice system, including arrest and sentencing disparities, reinforces a caste system of racial control that produces second-class citizens with fewer rights (Alexander, 2011; Lerman & Weaver, 2014). There is also an extensive literature on the numerous collateral consequences of involvement in the justice system, especially the adverse effects of monetary sanctions, which are most detrimental to disadvantaged populations and can contribute to re-offending as they accumulate (See Ostermann et al., 2024, for a review).

Police traffic stops offer the best example of how police enforcement has adverse effects on vulnerable populations. American law enforcement has placed enormous emphasis on "stop and frisk" as a tool for fighting crime (Meares, 2014; White & Fradella, 2016), but racial disparities in police decision-making during traffic stops have been documented repeatedly across dozens of agencies. Black drivers are stopped more often, stopped more often for nonsafety reasons ("pretextual stops"), searched more often, and subjected to force more often than white drivers (Graham, 2024; Graham et al., 2024; Langton & Durose, 2013; Pierson et al., 2020). Young Black and Hispanic males are particularly at risk of citations, searches, arrests, and use of force (Engel & Calnon, 2004). We must also recognize that traffic stops can be costly in other ways, such as the price of fines, fees, court summons, and incarceration, which can contribute to poverty (Alabama Appleseed Center for Law & Justice, 2023). Thus, the Center for Policing Equity has emphasized that the effects of police stops are compounding as "disparities at each step increase the risks of harm at subsequent decision points" (Graham, 2024, p. 1).

As a psychologist, I would like to underscore the fact that investigatory stops are embarrassing and upsetting for the drivers, who are often questioned and searched in front of family members, friends, or bystanders. As Epp and his colleagues (2014) document, drivers are often asked where they are going, why they need to go there, and what they are carrying in their glove compartment or trunk. Flashlights run through the windows in every conceivable section; people are asked to get out; personal items are strewn on the ground nearby. The psychological impact can be enormous, resulting in resentment, loss of trust, and growing anger toward the police, especially in communities of color.

In general, we now know from research that contact with the police can have adverse mental health consequences, especially for people of color, youth, and transgender populations (DeVylder et al., 2017). Police enforcement actions can have a range of adverse effects on youth, including increased school absentee-ism (Geller & Mark, 2022), increased recidivism (Klein, 1986), and reduced options for gainful employment (Bushway, 1996). These effects are especially large for young Black males, as they tend to be heavily policed, and thus hold very negative views of the police (Gau & Brunson, 2010; Geller, 2021; Suddler, 2019). The negative perceptions in the Black community are the result of both direct contact with the police (Tapp & Davis, 2022), and vicarious experience, such as conversations among friends and family (Rosenbaum et al., 2005).

Poor communities of color have long been the focus of police intrusion in large cities, as police seek to reduce crime. Unfortunately, we have known for half a century that police work often involves officers seeking to confirm their prejudicial suspicions about criminality (Rubinstein, 1973) and create a case of probable cause and enforcement using their own set of rules (Skolnick, 1975). Police are usually interacting with complete strangers, and in these settings, human beings feel a need to make snap judgments based on limited information – judgments that are often inaccurate (Gladwell, 2005). In general, people tend to attribute certain attitudes, beliefs, and behavioral traits to strangers (Baum et al., 1985), and this prejudice can lead to discrimination. For decades, psychologists have studied how we enhance our self-identity and preserve the status quo by using social stereotypes that emphasize the positive attributes of our "ingroup" while devaluing the attributes of the "outgroup" (Allport, 1954; McGarty et al., 2002; Tajfel & Turner, 1979). Today, we distinguish between "explicit" and "implicit" bias, with the understanding that all humans suffer from implicit bias that can lead to discrimination, and the police are no exception (see Fridell, 2008, 2017).

Today, with the increased polarization of political attitudes (Edsall, 2024), I am concerned about the national rise in expressions of prejudice toward outgroups and how this trend might affect police-community interactions. For example, we see a nationwide effort to abolish diversity, equity, and inclusion (D.E.I.) programs in education, as well as a broader anti-"wokeism" move-ment – organized efforts that run counter to social justice for all vulnerable groups (see Confessore, 2024). With the rise of homophobia, transphobia, antisemitism, xenophobia (around immigration), and other forms of prejudice, we must remember that police officers are susceptible to these attitudes as well. A study of 220,000 officers from 98 of the 100 largest local agencies found that police officers tend to be more conservative than the civilians they serve (Ba et al., 2023). Thus, those interested in changing police culture should be prepared for some backlash, such as the "Blue Lives Matter" movement, as well as the possibility of additional forms of discrimination.

Thus, to better understand the needs of all vulnerable and constitutionally protected classes, we need to consistently create space for them to voice their concerns and be prepared to hear about their interactions with the police. Furthermore, the community wants evidence that progress is being made to reduce these problems, as too much ambiguity remains about how to measure progress. Here, I will argue that, in the interest of impartial policing and transparency, cities should collect and publicize data on the quality of police services, with breakdowns by the demographic characteristics of the community members being served.

3.2 The Cost to Police Officers

My criticism here is focused largely on the failure of police reform, not on the majority of police officers who are simply trying to do a difficult job within their existing organizational structure. After four decades of observation, I fully understand that police work can be very difficult and it is made more difficult today because of the public outcry and calls for greater police accountability. On the job, officers can face violent and traumatic incidents that are hard to forget, from homicides to traffic fatalities to suicides. As a group, police officers are more likely to commit suicide than die on the job (Stanton, 2022), and they have a suicide rate higher than civilians (McAward, 2022). The national trend to introduce officer wellness programs (U.S. Department of Justice, 2024) is a clear indication of the stressfulness of police work. Hopefully, the new management model proposed here will help to reduce some of the stress of police work.

4 The Ineffectiveness of Police Reform

From crime commissions to consent decrees, the United States has sought to increase police accountability and transparency for nearly a century. Some improvements have been noted (Skogan & Frydl, 2004), but the general mistreatment of the public remains problematic. We have summarized the problem in one sentence: "American policing progressed from an unregulated politicized entity that eventually enforced 'Jim Crow' laws to an organized, quasi-military bureaucracy focused on law enforcement" (Rosenbaum & McCarty, 2017, p. 71).

The reforms led by August Vollmer and O. W. Wilson in the twentieth century were designed to insulate the police from long-standing corruption and improve effectiveness in fighting crime. I have summarized the professional model of policing in this way: "Uniforms, military ranks, written policies and procedures, centralized control and command, highly trained specialized units (including detectives), motorized patrols, and modern technology were expected to eliminate corruption, professionalize the police, and above all, prevent crime through rapid response, random patrol, and forensic investigations" (Rosenbaum, 2007, p. 14). This professional model seems to have reduced corruption, but has been ineffective in fighting crime or building police legitimacy. Within this framework, police organizations have used symbols, dress, and ceremonies to maintain their legitimacy and promote their image and values as fair, professional crime fighters (Crank & Langworthy, 1992; Gau, 2014). However, as Gau (2014) notes, these images and values "are decoupled from task performance," and thus are essentially myths created to ensure police legitimacy.

In fact, this detached, quasi-military model of policing has contributed directly to the crisis of legitimacy that continues to fester. From Rodney King in 1991 to Tyre Nichols in 2023, the beatings and deaths have continued and calls for police reform have intensified (e.g., Balko, 2014; Morrison et al., 2023). The typical requests for more "accountability" and "transparency" will be insufficient. I am pleased that the Police Executive Research Forum (PERF) has established new guidelines for police use of force, especially when restraining persons who are having a medical, mental, or drug crisis (Seewer & Dunklin, 2024), but I remain skeptical that these guidelines will significantly change behavior on the streets without changes to the police culture and performance standards.

For decades, policing scholars have associated excessive force and mistreatment of the public with this militaristic culture and the war-like mentality used to combat crime and drugs (e.g., Skolnick, 1975; Skolnick & Fyfe, 1993). Yes, there are a few rotten apples, but mistreatment of the public by a large segment of the police force is associated with the social norms within the police culture. Psychological and physical training to be a warrior with a "bulletproof mind" is important for surviving in battle (Grossman & Christensen, 2008), but the job of police officers is very different. Most police officers never fire their weapon during their entire career and attempts to kill them are extremely rare. Yet the training for new police recruits in the United States exposes them to videos showing officers being ambushed or killed during traffic stops (Kirkpatrick et al., 2021), reinforcing the mindset of being hypervigilant and suspicious of everyone they encounter. Academy evaluations with pretests and posttests have shown that recruits develop a significantly greater desire to use physical force to solve problems and have less respect toward the community after six months of training (Rosenbaum & Lawrence, 2017). Another pre–post study found that recruits become more inclined to believe that police misconduct and the code of silence are less serious problems after academy training (Schuck & Rabe-Hemp, 2021). Thus, from the start, the socialization process strengthens their cultural identity as tough warriors who must be on guard against hostile community members, demand obedience, use force to solve problems, and maintain secrecy within the group. Too often, this socialization process undermines, rather than builds, community trust.

Thus, police reform must directly confront this culture and style of policing to achieve widespread public trust. In this Element, I argue that the focus and priorities of police organizations must change. Lum and Nagin (2017) make a compelling case that policing in a democratic society should be built on two basic principles. The first is that crime prevention should be prioritized over arrests, consistent with Peelian principles. The second is that "citizens' views about the police and their tactics for preventing crime and disorder matter independently of police effectiveness" (p. 339). The authors contend that these two principles are equally important and "neither has standing to trump the other." Consistent with Lum and Nagin's conclusion, I am calling on reformers and police researchers to acknowledge the importance of public perceptions of the police and do something about it to advance knowledge and "evidence-based policing" (cf. Sherman, 2013). My position is also consistent with Klose's (2024) revised definition of evidence-based policing that includes "community values, preferences, and circumstances" in the decision-making process.

Since the 1980s, there have been many reforms and innovations in policing (Rosenbaum, 2007). Most of these reforms have been ineffective and some even harmful. I will give some attention to reforms that are relevant to the organizational and research agenda proposed here, seeking to give more attention to policing processes rather than policing outcomes, although the two can be, and should be, connected.

Since the death of George Floyd, there have been nearly 300 state laws that seek to reform the police in various ways, including more civilian oversight, limitations on use of force, anti-bias training, and alternatives to arrest in mental health cases (Monnay, 2022). There has been considerable pushback by law enforcement personnel against these changes, and the general focus of these reforms is the misuse of force, not other police-public interactions.

4.1 Police Accountability and Public Safety

Individual cities have tried to control behavior through discipline and even firing officers for misconduct, but with little success. For most agencies, less than 10 percent of the misconduct complaints are investigated (Kelly & Nichols, 2020). The cases investigated by Internal Affairs are usually cleared and police reports often lack important details. When deaths are involved, officers are usually exonerated by reports from medical examiners and coroners (Dunklin et al., 2024). When punishments are recommended, strong union contracts allow appeals to arbitration, which rarely result in sanctions. In one *New York Times* review, roughly half of the fired officers were reinstated (Barker et al., 2021). Even most police officers agree that accountability systems are not working. In our national survey of more than 13,000 police officers in 89 large agencies, only 1 in 5 officers felt that "officers who do a poor job are held accountable" (Cordner, 2017). With qualified immunity, police officers are not financially responsible for their misconduct (Yancey-Bragg, 2023). Furthermore, thousands of officers who have been fired by one agency are rehired by another, as decertification systems are rarely in place (Stecklow, 2024).

Although ineffective, this entire process, including public outcry, leaves many officers feeling mistreated, which affects their work-related attitudes and behavior. Our national survey found that when officers are upset about organizational injustice, such as unfair discipline, they are less committed to organizational goals, express less job satisfaction, and are less willing to comply with agency rules (Rosenbaum & McCarty, 2017). In the larger context of anti-police sentiment in the media and public protests, many police officers have become demoralized (Bello, 2014). In a national survey, police officers expressed anger toward the public and fear of being unfairly disciplined or fired (Pew Research Center, 2017). These sentiments resulted in significant "de-policing" after the George Floyd protests in 2020 (Nix et al., 2024). Today, many police prefer to "lay low" and avoid unnecessary risks, which can reduce public safety. For example, in New Jersey, a huge drop in traffic-related citations by the state police (due to criticism of their agency) was followed by a dramatic increase in traffic accidents (Tully, 2024). Thus, we can see how police behavior and public safety can be negatively influenced when reforms are not handled properly. Later, I will revisit the issue of police effectiveness in fighting crime.

The complaints filed by community members provide insight into police-public interactions and how these encounters can escalate. One of the most common complaints is that the officer was discourteous, including used offensive language (e.g., Seron et al., 2006; Terrill and Reisig, 2003). But as Seron and colleagues (2006) note after reviewing complaints against the New York Police, "alleged misconduct often escalates into behavior that is asserted as having been abusive or unnecessarily forceful" (p. 928). This might include verbally threatening civilians or using force ranging from pushing to beating. Research has shown that police respond in a punitive manner when civilians fail to comply or are judged to be disrespectful of police authority (Klinger, 1997; Mastrofski et al., 2002; Worden & Shepard, 1996). The real problem is that, aside from these few studies, we know very little about what transpires during daily police-public encounters in American cities. Here I propose to fix this problem.

After negative media coverage of deadly force incidents, many police agencies have tried to increase accountability by changing their use of force policies, conducting more thorough internal investigations of these incidents, creating early intervention systems (EIS) to identify officers at risk, and offering new training on when force is appropriate. While these reforms have been helpful in some ways (see Walker & Archbold, 2020), they have serious limitations. There are many reasons why these internal changes have had limited impact on street-level policing and public trust, including internal resistance to change, a lack of expertise needed to analyze data, deficiencies in data quality, lack of objectivity when evaluating other officers, weak training, and administrative turnover.

Early intervention systems (EIS) programs are now popular and have potential for identifying and intervening with officers who are at risk of misconduct (Walker & Archbold, 2020). However, we do not have a standard set of metrics to define "at risk," and those currently used are not good predictors of problematic behaviors (Russek & Fitzpatrick, 2021; Worden et al., 2014). As La Vigne (2022) notes, even if EIS uses fancy algorithms to identify patterns, relying on existing police records will lead to "garbage in, garbage out." My own experience as a consent decree monitor suggests that EIS personnel are forced to rely on their own judgment or "rules of thumb" rather than "predictive analytics." Also, supervisors are often free to do whatever they want to satisfy the requirements of an EIS intervention. Often, they do very little beyond having a brief talk with the officer.

I want to point out that focusing on the behavior of a few "rotten apples" doesn't help us understand the problematic behavior patterns of a larger segment of the police force as shown in contact surveys. To be clear, excessive force incidents are extremely rare, and minor force incidents often go unreported due to the "code of silence" or they are reported with justification from the officer's perspective. Furthermore, the civilians who file complaints are not representative of the much larger group of unhappy service recipients who are afraid of police retaliation. Thus, a much broader set of performance metrics with predictive validity is needed, including metrics that give greater voice to the community and metrics that rely on indisputable video data.

Existing training is also problematic for police reform. More than a half century ago, following the crisis of legitimacy in the 1960s, psychologists were critical of the standard police training programs and proposed an approach that would focus on "basic skills of being helpful to another" (Danish & Ferguson, 1973, p. 499), but little progress followed. Today, a few hours of classroom training on de-escalation and proper communication is a drop in the bucket. A nationwide survey found that recruits in state and local law enforcement training academies receive an average of 168 hours of training on firearms, self-defense, and use of force, compared to only 10 hours on communication and 8 hours on ethics and integrity (Reaves, 2016). In addition to a stronger "dosage" of training on these topics, we need new community-based metrics to assess the impact of training on job performance.

Performance evaluations conducted by supervisors are also problematic and lack credibility. Researchers have recommended ways to improve performance evaluations (e.g., Oettmeier & Wycoff, 1997), but the reality is that police work is largely unsupervised. Supervisors are rarely present during most police encounters with the public, and with new BWC data, a few agencies are requiring supervisors to review only a small and unrepresentative sample of footage. Also, performance is difficult to evaluate with existing police records, which have little to do with the quality of police service overall and are based on selective community complaints and use of force incidents. Even when agencies require supervisors to evaluate the quality of police service by individual officers, the results are not credible without observational data to validate these judgments. Furthermore, for decades, the police culture has encouraged supervisors to be loyal to their officers (Engel, 2001) and protect them from criticism by headquarters (Skolnick & Fyfe, 1993). For example, after reviewing more than 2,000 ratings of performance in one large police department, I discovered that supervisors never once gave a rating of "Needs Improvement" on any of the dozens of performance metrics. How are officers supposed to improve their performance if they don't receive any helpful feedback? Anecdotally, I have asked many officers today how they are evaluated, and the typical response is "Whether I can stay out of trouble."

External civilian oversight and auditing have been recommended for years (Mastrofski, 1999; Reiss, 1971), and have potential, but they are usually opposed by the police and lack critical data needed to accurately evaluate police performance (Walker & Archbold, 2020). Also, the composition and expertise of these groups is sometimes questionable. Nevertheless, civilian oversight is needed in some capacity, as articulated in this publication.

Beginning in the 1990s, consent decrees by the US Department of Justice have required that police agencies correct a "pattern or practice" of unconstitutional policing against protected groups. While these legal agreements have resulted in some improvements to policies and training regarding the use of force in more than forty agencies involved (US Department of Justice, 2017; Lawrence & Cole, 2019; Walker, 2017), thousands of police agencies without consent decrees are not required to make these changes. Sometimes, the force training involves teaching officers to include in their force reports that "I feared for my life." These consent decrees are not only very costly but they are also slow to get started and typically drag on for years because of failure to comply fully with the terms of the agreement (Ravani, 2022) or because of local opposition and national politics (Lynch & Goudsward, 2024). Reaching beyond the focus of consent decrees, here I will emphasize the need for additional changes in accountability and performance assessments that have a better chance of influencing police behavior on the street and thus enhancing police legitimacy.

4.2 Key Innovations in Policing

Various innovations have been proposed to either fight crime more effectively and/or enhance police legitimacy. Most police work since the 1960s has been reactive, namely, responding to calls, taking reports and conducting investigations of crimes already committed. However, since the 1980s, innovation in policing has transitioned to more proactive attempts to prevent crime and engage the community. Here I take a quick look at some of the main strategies and why they have largely failed to change the style of policing or the police culture.

4.2.1 Community Policing

Many reform efforts were introduced in the 1980s to address the legitimacy problem through community engagement and community policing (Cordner, 1997; Green & Mastrofski, 1988; Rosenbaum, 1988, 1994; Skogan & Hartnett, 1997). Community policing remains very popular, but the obstacles to full-scale implementation have been numerous (see Fridell & Wycoff, 2004; Mirzer, 1996; Skogan, 2003). Community policing initiatives were conceived primarily as community relations programs to demonstrate police interest in community concerns, but they were never fully integrated into the daily practice of policing. Furthermore, observational studies in Chicago (Skogan & Hartnett, 1997), Seattle (Lyons, 1999), and Los Angeles (Gascon & Roussell, 2019) have documented how these programs can be insensitive to many of the concerns raised by community members. Although community policing programs remain very popular, neither the structure nor the function of American police organizations has changed significantly as a result of these initiatives (Maguire, 1997; Mastrofski, 2019).

4.2.2 Problem-Oriented Policing

Also emerging in the 1980s was problem-oriented policing (POP), pioneered by Herman Goldstein (1979, 1990). Goldstein argued that the time has come for police to focus on solving crime-related problems and addressing their causes, rather than being obsessed with incident-driven, law enforcement actions such as making arrests. Eck and Spelman (1987) articulated a four-step process to implement POP called the SARA model (Scanning to identify the problem, Analysis to collect information about the problem, Response to implement solutions, and Assessment to evaluate effectiveness). Problem-oriented policing was a great idea, but the management structure did not change to support this approach to policing. As Braga and Weisburd (2019) note, "it seems unrealistic to expect line-level officers to conduct in-depth problem-oriented policing" (p. 198) without the support of researchers and administrators. Furthermore, POP has focused on reducing crime and disorder problems, but rarely other problems that concern the community. Nevertheless, the most rigorous evaluations suggest that intensive POP with full organizational support can produce short-term reductions in crime and disorder (Hinkle et al., 2020; Weisburd & Majmundar, 2018). In the present context, however, POP has failed to address the problem of public anger and distrust of the police, and police agencies have failed to adequately seek or respond to community feedback on this issue. Nevertheless, I see the SARA model as very applicable to the organizational changes outlined in Section 7.2.3, with the goal of increasing police legitimacy.

4.2.3 Information Technology and Outcome-Based Policing

Policing in the twenty-first century can be viewed as "the Information Technology era" (Rosenbaum, 2007) because of the focus on geo-based crime-fighting and the surveillance of suspects with the aid of computers. Multiple technologies are being used to predict and fight crime, including body-worn cameras (BWCs), data mining systems, heat sensors, biometrics, nonlethal weapons, GPS tracking, electronic monitoring, telecommunication systems, Internet searches, facial recognition software, drones, and data analytics with artificial intelligence.

The public has complained about secrecy and the lack of transparency in police work for many years. Body-worn cameras represent a significant attempt to address this concern using technology (White, 2014), allowing us to see what happens during police-public encounters. However, a large body of research has failed to identify stable effects of BWCs on the behavior of police officers or community members, with the exception of a reduction in community complaints (Lum et al., 2019, 2020). Furthermore, the original BWC goals of transparency and accountability have not been achieved at the organizational level. Videos tend to be reviewed by Internal Affairs only when an incident involves a serious public complaint, high level of use of force, or an officer-involved shooting – estimated at less than 1 percent of all encounters. For the other 99 percent, the millions of hours of BWC footage remain untouched.

However, BWC data have changed the ball game by introducing a totally new source of evidence about what transpired during police-public encounters. As I will stress in this publication, BWC data has great potential for identifying patterns of behavior that contribute to, or undermine, public trust and confidence in the police. Such data can also be used to understand why force or violence occurs in some face-to-face interactions, but not in others.

One of the original pillars of the information technology revolution was CompStat, introduced in the New York Police Department in 1994 (Bratton, 1999; Walsh, 2001). With computers used to analyze crime patterns, New York's CompStat model became extremely popular. Arguably, this was the first time that police managers were held accountable for performance on the street, but unfortunately, it encouraged an increase in traditional methods of aggressive, reactive policing to improve the crime statistics in each district. It also encouraged a punitive environment within the organization, which encouraged dishonesty in reporting performance data. Most importantly, CompStat systems failed to gauge in any meaningful way the quality of policing – only the volume of law enforcement activities and crime statistics for large geographic areas.

Given the calls for greater transparency and community voice in policing, the Vera Institute and the National Policing Institute sought to upgrade the CompStat model with a national conference in 2016 and a series of papers to follow in 2018 (Shah et al., 2018). Acknowledging the original criticism of CompStat (e.g., Willis et al., 2010), the recommendations for "CompStat 2.0" sought to incorporate community policing (with regular meetings between the police and community stakeholders), incorporate problem-oriented policing (with a broader focus on identifying and addressing local problems), and expand performance measures beyond crime statistics to problem-solving. Unfortunately, the quality of police services and the treatment of individual community members by the police was not given much attention.

Since the 1990s, other police innovations have since competed for dominance, including broken windows policing, hot spots policing, pulling levers policing, predictive policing, and specialty unit policing, with most of these aided by advances in information technology to target geo-based hot spots of crime and disorder or individuals (see Weisburd & Braga, 2006). Controlled experiments have taught us that hot spots policing is one of the few policing strategies that is effective in reducing crime (Braga et al., 2019; Weisburd & Braga, 2019; Weisburd & Eck, 2017), at least for short periods of time. However, I have argued that this wave of geo-targeted policing strategies tends to be aggressive and inequitable as practiced by most police agencies (Rosenbaum, 1993, 2007, 2019). A recent National Academies (2025) workshop on the use of predictive policing approaches cautioned police regarding the potential risk of disparate impact and violations of civil liberties, and the need for a more holistic approach that gives attention to community trust as well as crime reduction.

Because of the focus on aggressive enforcement, these "outcome-based performance models" are more likely to undermine public trust in the police, especially in minority and marginalized communities, than "process-based policing models" (Tyler, 2005). Hence, this Element focuses on advancing knowledge and practice of process-based policing, and, where appropriate, linking it to outcome-based policing models, as Weisburd and his colleagues have done (Weisburd et al., 2022).

4.2.4 Traffic Stops and Public Safety

Since the late 1990s, American police organizations have believed that stopping, questioning, and frisking (SQF) individuals is the most effective method of achieving their primary goal of reducing crime. If weapons, drugs, and other contraband can be recovered and criminals can be stopped and arrested, this will reduce crime (For details on these tactics, see Remsberg, 1995). However, the widespread adoption of this proactive enforcement strategy stems, in large part, from a misinterpretation of research on hot spots policing, where studies found that such police interventions can be effective in reducing crime *when* applied to very small geographic areas or "hot spots" (Weisburd & Braga, 2019; Weisburd & Eck, 2017). The success of the pioneering Kansas City Gun Experiment (Sherman & Weisburd, 1995), with four officers intensely producing stops, citations, and arrests on specific street segments of one district, received widespread attention. As a result, many police organizations dramatically increased stops in entire neighborhoods, precincts, or large areas – a bad translation of evidence-based policing and one that leads to many good people feeling harassed by intrusive police tactics. In the United States, we have reached a point where police make roughly 50,000 traffic stops per day or 20 million per year (Baumgartner et al., 2018).

Many of these stops are "pretextual stops" for minor violations, such as a broken taillight or tinted windows, which are employed to ask additional questions and make observations to justify a search of the vehicle or person for evidence of criminal activity (Graham, 2024). These investigatory stops require "reasonable suspicion" that the person has committed or is in the process of committing a crime. However, research clearly indicates that (1) these stops are more common and include more enforcement against Black drivers (Graham, 2024; Graham et al., 2024; Langton & Durose, 2013; Pierson et al., 2020); (2) "reasonable suspicion" is often lacking before the search is conducted (Skogan, 2023); (3) hit rates for finding contraband are very low and officers are less likely to seize contraband from Black drivers than white drivers (e.g., Engel & Calnon, 2004; Lofstrom et al., 2022; Pierson et al., 2020; Weiss & Rosenbaum, 2009); (4) mental and physical health effects on community members can be substantial (as noted earlier); and, perhaps most importantly, (5) traffic stops are ineffective at controlling crime, whether conducted in the United States (McCann, 2023) or England and Wales (Tiratelli et al., 2018), and thus waste substantial police resources that could be devoted to other crime-fighting methods.

Gladwell (2019) illustrates this last point very clearly using the North Carolina State Highway Patrol as an example. Learning of this new approach to fighting crime, the agency increased its traffic stops from 400,000 to 800,000 over seven years. Gladwell reports that 400,000 searches resulted in only 17 cases where guns or drugs were recovered, begging the question, "[i]s it really worth alienating and stigmatizing 399,983 [drivers] . . . to find 17 bad apples?" (p. 337). Thus, these pretextual stops rarely produce anything that could be helpful in solving crimes and most are irrelevant to traffic safety. Stops for speeding, drunk driving, or running traffic lights would be a much better use of officers' time, or devoting these hours to more effective crime prevention work. In fact, unarmed drivers who are not being pursued for a violent crime are killed at a rate of more than one per week (Kirkpatrick et al., 2021).

The damage to police image can be consequential. The national contact survey shows that Black and Hispanic drivers are less likely than whites to believe that the reason for their stop was legitimate (Langton & Durose, 2013). This perceived lack of fairness can place an upper limit on the level of cooperation and compliance that can be expected from the public, which, in turn, has serious consequences for public safety. Consistent harassment and perceived lack of fairness can contribute to legal cynicism in the community (Kirk & Papachristos, 2011), which can undermine public safety. Thus, we need to systematically measure how vulnerable groups feel about their encounters.

Pedestrian stops are also controversial. These proactive crime control programs have stimulated an important debate among academics about the costs and benefits of the common policing tactic of SQF when applied to pedestrians (Ratcliffe et al., 2024). Some argue it should be used only to reduce gun violence in high-crime neighborhoods, but these tend to be neighborhoods of color (Kegler et al., 2023). Weisburd and his colleagues (Petersen et al., 2023; Weisburd et al., 2023) conducted a Campell Collaborative Systematic Review of pedestrian stops. While these SQFs reduced crime (roughly 13 percent), they also were associated with mental and physical harm to the community members who were stopped, as well as more negative views of the police and increased delinquency. Consequently, the authors of the review concluded that "existing scientific evidence does not support the widespread use of SQFs as a proactive policing strategy" (p. 2). The concerns about SQFs, including adverse legitimacy effects, not only suggest the need for more dialogue with the community about SQF tactics (see Sherman, 2023) but also underscores the need for new systems of measurement that will allow researchers to monitor the impact of policing practices.

4.2.5 Responding to Persons with Mental Illness

In response to police killing or mistreating persons suffering from mental illness, many police departments have introduced training programs for officers. Crisis Intervention Teams (CIT), based on the 1988 "Memphis Model," have spread rapidly across the United States, with some good police training to de-escalate tension with individuals facing a mental health crisis (Watson et al., 2019). However, management has inadequate mechanisms in place to ensure that the behaviors being recommended in training have translated into street-level behaviors. Even the Memphis Police Department has been accused by the U.S. Department of Justice of unlawfully discriminating against people with behavioral health disabilities (Department of Justice, 2024).

Given the proven danger of armed police responding to mental health crises, we have witnessed a national movement to create community responder programs that employ unarmed public officials to handle nonviolent mental health calls for service (Beckett et al., 2021). I am supportive of these programs, but there is much work to be done to decide which calls they are qualified to handle and how they will interact with the police. One famous policing scholar argued that the primary function of the police is to handle situations that require "coercive force" (Bittner, 1970), that is, when someone needs to be restrained with force or is judged to be a threat to someone else's safety. However, these are rare calls for service, and the unarmed community responders are not prepared to handle all remaining nonforce incidents. Thus, we still need to more directly address the problem of how to produce a kinder, gentler, and more empathetic response from police officers.

4.3 Summary of Past Reforms

We have witnessed dozens of strategies to reform police organizations over the past century, including one of my favorites, community policing. Unfortunately, these interventions have achieved little success at changing police culture or police behavior on the streets. Despite all the new attention on managing use of force, the number of fatal police shootings continues to increase, reaching a record high of more than 1,200 deaths in 2023 (Washington Post, 2024). Also, the 378 police officers shot in the line of duty in 2023 is the highest in history (National Fraternal Order of Police, 2024).

To make matters worse, the public is both critical of aggressive crime-fighting and, at the same time, asking for more enforcement. This happened in the 1980s with drug enforcement (Rosenbaum, 1993), and is happening again with cities and states returning to "tough on crime" policies and increasing police powers (Hernandez, 2024), despite overall declines in crime. This includes recriminalizing drug activity in public places, returning to pretextual traffic stops, and arresting the growing homeless population for camping in public spaces (e.g., Hernandez, 2024; VanSickle, 2024; Woolington & Lewis, 2018).

Unfortunately, the growth in rigid bureaucratic controls and external criticism of the police seems to have increased police solidarity and their psychological distance from the communities they serve. Research on group dynamics reminds us that external threat leads to internal group cohesion (Lang et al., 2021). Today, we see "de-policing" to "stay out of trouble," along with negative attitudes toward the community being served.

Here I make the argument that progress in police organizations has been restricted by failure to explore new measures of performance and new methods of accountability that are less punitive, grounded in social science knowledge, and give attention to the community's voice when evaluating police services.

5 Measuring What Matters to the Community

What do we mean by "good policing?" The police mission is "to serve and protect" and the public would like a better definition of "to serve." To achieve marked improvements in public satisfaction with police performance, others have joined me in making the argument that performance metrics must be expanded to incorporate new measures of the quality of policing as defined by the community (Engel & Eck, 2015; Langworthy, 1999; Lum & Nagin, 2017; Mastrofski, 1999; McCarthy & Rosenbaum, 2015; Moore et al., 2002). For many years, the limitations of traditional measures of performance have been well documented in the scholarly literature (Alpert & Moore, 1993; Blumstein, 1999; Goldstein, 1990; Grant & Terry, 2005; Maguire, 2004a; Masterson & Stevens, 2002; Moore & Poethig, 1999; Moore et al., 2002; Reisig, 1999; Skolnick & Fyfe, 1993; Sparrow, 2015; White, 2007). Official statistics, such as reported crime rates, clearance rates, citations, arrests, and other enforcement activities, not only suffer from inaccuracy, but more importantly, they provide a very incomplete picture of police work. Within the framework of policing in a democratic society, police scholars and practitioners have called for greater attention to policing *processes* rather than policing *outcomes* (Mastrofski, 1999; Moore et al., 2002). Specifically, traditional measures fail to capture what is most important to the public, namely, how they are treated by the police. Thus, policing scholars have called upon the field to "measure what matters" to the community (Dunworth et al., 2000; Langworthy, 1999; Masterson & Stevens 2002; Mastrofski, 1999; Rosenbaum, 2004). What matters most is procedural justice.

5.1 Procedural Justice

In the pursuit of evidence-based policing, we should use public satisfaction with police encounters, and the sense of procedural justice that drives this satisfaction, as core metrics to define "good policing." The pioneering work of Tom Tyler and his colleagues (Lind & Tyler, 1988; Tyler, 1990; Tyler & Huo, 2002) has paved the way for numerous studies in many countries showing that people's judgments about the police and police legitimacy are heavily influenced by their sense of whether the process is fair and the officer's behavior is appropriate (Bradford, 2014; Bradford et al., 2014; Hough et al., 2013; Mazerolle et al., 2014; Quattlebaum et al., 2018; Tankebe, 2013; Tyler, 2004; Tyler & Fagan, 2008). Although community residents want safer streets and less violence, most importantly, they want a police force that is fair and sensitive to their needs (Rosenbaum et al., 2005; Skogan & Frydl, 2004; Tyler, 2005; Weitzer & Tuch, 2005).

When evaluating police performance from the public's perspective, the police response to crime incidents should be placed in the larger context of daily police work. In ten cities examined by the *New York Times*, serious violent crime comprised only about 1 percent of the calls for service (Asher & Horwitz, 2021). In nine cities, the Vera Institute of Justice found that less than 3 percent of all 911 emergency calls involved violent crime situations and only 37 percent involved any type of criminal activity (Dholakia, 2022). Hence, the detached crime-fighting model has little relevance to the vast majority of calls for service, yet the treatment of the public during these noncrime situations remains very important to their assessment of police legitimacy and public cooperation. For example, the traffic stop is the most common method of police-public contact and, as described earlier, it is a setting where multiple problems can develop regarding fair and respectful treatment.

I will acknowledge here that some policing scholars have debated whether there is a causal link between procedural justice and police legitimacy, given that most studies are correlational and do not involve experimental designs (e.g., Nagin & Telep, 2017). I acknowledge this issue, but simply point out that procedural justice, legitimacy, and many other human perceptions have been strongly linked in hundreds of studies (for a review, see Tyler & Nobo, 2022), and that causality has been demonstrated in one randomized trial (Jonathan-Zamir et al., 2024). Also, researchers have used a "subjective causality approach" by conducting in-depth interviews of protestors and concluded that the fairness of treatment influences their judgments of police legitimacy and not the reverse (Perry et al., 2023).

Another debated issue is whether procedural justice should be given priority over fighting crime. I want to emphasize that this is not a "zero-sum game" or trade-off. We don't need to pick between procedural justice and public safety, and others agree with me (Engel & Eck, 2015). The police should continue to fight crime but do so in a manner that is less harmful to the community. In addition, we have reason to believe that procedural justice and crime control are connected. We know from many studies that when the police act in a procedurally just manner, the public is more likely to view the police as legitimate and trustworthy (Donner et al., 2015), less cynical about the law (Gau, 2015), more likely to obey the law (Tyler, 1990), and more likely to cooperate with the police (Maguire & Lowrey, 2017; Murphy & Cherney, 2012; Rosenbaum et al., 2017; Tyler, 2004, 2006). This also means the community is more likely to comply with police requests (Walters & Bolger, 2018), thus avoiding the need to use force, and is more likely to cooperate by reporting criminal activity (Bolger & Walters, 2019).

Perhaps the most compelling evidence of the linkage between procedural justice and crime comes from a study by Weisburd and his colleagues (2022) in three cities where officers were randomly assigned to hot spots with or without five days of procedural justice training. Officers in the training condition showed more respectful treatment of community members, made fewer arrests, and received fewer perceptions of police harassment and violence than officers in the control group. Most importantly, there was a significant relative 14 percent reduction in crime incidents in the experimental hot spots where officers received the procedural justice training.

Procedurally just behaviors by the police should contribute to more complete and effective investigations of crime due to increased cooperation, thus contributing to deterrence. Also, when the public views the police as trustworthy, they are more likely to exhibit community engagement and collective efficacy (Tyler & Meares, 2021). A community's "collective efficacy" and "willingness to intervene" are associated with lower levels of neighborhood violence and less fear of crime (Sampson et al., 1997). For these reasons, I have repeatedly encouraged the "co-production" of public safety by engaging community members in crime prevention and multiagency partnerships (Rosenbaum, 1986, 2002; Rosenbaum et al., 1998; Schuck & Rosenbaum, 2006).

The police could use more help from the community in fighting crime. Clearance rates are low and have continued to decline over the ten-year period beginning in 2013 (Gramlich, 2024). Police now clear only 52 percent of homicides, 41 percent of aggravated assaults, and 23 percent of robberies. Clearance rates for rape have declined dramatically from 41 percent to 26 percent during this period. If public trust in the police were higher, we could expect greater public cooperation in solving crime and weaken the "No Snitch" culture present in many high-crime neighborhoods.

For this Element, the key elements of procedural justice need to be defined (for an introduction, see President's Task Force on 21st Century Policing, 2015; Rosenbaum et al., 2017; Yale Law School Justice Collaboratory, 2023). Essentially, procedural justice research shows that the public's perceptions of police are strongly influenced by the quality of their encounter with the police. Tyler and other policing scholars have identified four key components of procedural justice when interacting with the police:

(1) *Dignity and Respect*: Are community members treated with dignity and respect by the officers?
(2) *Voice*: Are community members given a voice or chance to express their concerns? Are they allowed to participate in the decision-making process?
(3) *Neutrality*: Are the officers neutral or unbiased in their decisions, guided by consistent and transparent reasons? Are decisions based on the facts and legal procedures, rather than personal biases about race/ethnicity, gender, age, sexual orientation, mental health, religion, or other factors that are not legally relevant?
(4) *Trustworthiness*: Are the officers conveying trustworthy motives and showing concern about the well-being of those who are affected by their decisions?

These components can be combined into a single Procedural Justice (PJ) Index, as we did under the National Police Research Platform with fifty-eight agencies. As you can see from Figures 1 and 2, the larger the agency, the lower the procedural justice ratings received by officers and the lower the overall public satisfaction with the encounter. Thus, the problem of procedural injustice is greater in larger, urban areas with larger crime problems and more diversity. Across all agencies, procedural justice reported by white residents on four key measures was roughly 12 percentage points higher than Black residents and 8 percentage points higher than Hispanic residents.

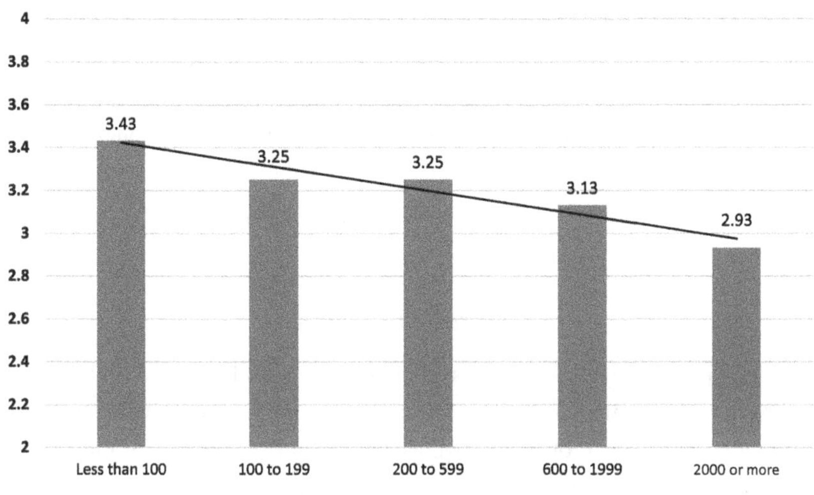

Figure 1 Overall procedural justice index.

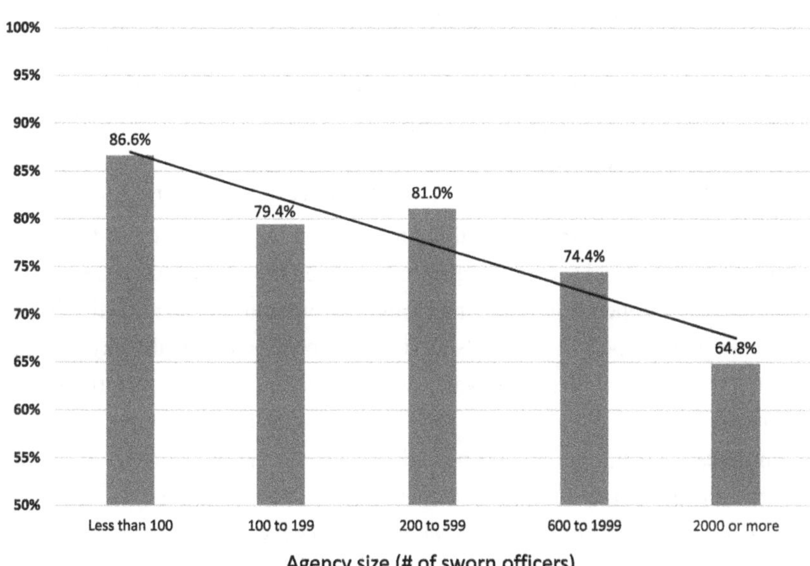

Figure 2 Overall satisfaction by agency size. (% satisfied and very satisfied).

Next I will review research in the social sciences that underscores the importance of each of these components, and how interpersonal communication skills are the key to successful procedural justice in practice. The systems proposed here should be able to measure the main components of procedural justice by capturing relevant information from verbal and nonverbal behavior.

The importance of this interpersonal communication should be clear – it can lead to the escalation of conflict and use of force or to mutual respect, trust, and cooperation. After reviewing the scientific literature on police programs seeking to improve police legitimacy, Mazerolle and colleagues (2013a) concluded that frontline procedurally just communication with the public "is important for promoting citizen satisfaction, confidence, compliance and cooperation with the police."

5.1.1 Respectful Treatment

All human beings have a strong psychological need to be treated with dignity and respect. Regardless of the circumstances, no one wants to be embarrassed, humiliated, demeaned, or dismissed, especially in the presence of others. We know from social psychology that this motivation stems from our desire to maintain a positive social identity and self-esteem (Lind & Tyler, 1988). Interactions that are not respectful and threaten our self-identity will not be received positively.

Respectful treatment can be understood in the context of interpersonal communication, where each action usually causes a reaction. Communication is often received with positive or negative emotional reactions. Social psychologists have identified the social norms of positive and negative reciprocity (Gouldner, 1960). According to the positive reciprocity norm, you are expected to respond to a positive action with another positive action. In other words, when someone says or does something nice to you, usually there is a feeling of gratitude, and you feel a need to repay them, which then contributes to equity in relationships, cooperation, and other positive outcomes (Chen et al., 2009). Conversely, if the person responds to you in a negative or hostile way, you are inclined to respond in the same way – which is called negative reciprocity.

I have observed both positive and negative reciprocity in police-public communication, and the latter can easily lead to escalation of tensions. Many officers are trained to believe that their legal authority and power does not require them to play by these social rules. However, the adverse effects of disrespect are clear – research shows that when someone is disrespected by the police, they typically respond in a negative manner, exhibiting disobedience and resistance (Terrill & Reisig, 2003).

Similarly, holding stereotypes can often lead to disrespectful treatment by the police. I have already discussed racial bias in enforcement. No one wants to be questioned, searched, and treated as if they are a suspected criminal, which happens too often in high-crime neighborhoods where the vast majority of residents are law-abiding community members. This well-documented reality may help to explain the results of a meta-analysis by Bolger and colleagues (2021), which found that satisfaction with the police is lower for people of color, younger people, and those who have been victims of crime.

Interpersonal communication skills are critical for giving and receiving respect. Routinely, police officers interview victims, suspects, and bystanders to gather information, but there are good and bad methods of interviewing and procedural justice is essential. Considerable scientific knowledge regarding effective interviewing techniques can be applied to police work (Stewart & Cash, 2008).

One study offers some insight regarding effective police communication styles when interacting with suspects. Foster and colleagues (2024) analyzed 438 BWCs and dashcam video recordings from two police agencies. They found that when patrol officers "presented a positive tenor/demeanor or employed noncoercive verbal tactics," suspects were significantly more likely to comply with their requests. In contrast, officers' use of "coercive verbal tactics or accusatory language" did not improve compliance levels. Furthermore, such negative communication may escalate the tension and lead to use of force, but will certainly lower procedural justice evaluations.

When evaluating police-public interactions, I also emphasize the importance of basic conversational etiquette for gaining respect. As you know, etiquette is a set of rules or practices endorsed by society regarding appropriate behavior in interpersonal settings (e.g., Muja, 2014; Sia, 2023). All social interactions should have a beginning, middle, and end. The conversation should have a beginning where you identify yourself and greet the person, a middle where you listen and wait your turn to talk ("turn taking"), and an ending, where you close the conversation by saying something like "thank you" or "take care." Differential power dynamics can also cause officers to skip over some of the social etiquette requirements that are normally expected in social exchanges, thus undermining procedural justice.

Importantly, when you realize that something is not going right in a conversation (e.g., the other person has been offended), you engage in "conversation repair" (Albert & De Ruiter, 2018), such as "I'm sorry I interrupted you – go ahead and finish what you were saying about your neighbor" or "I'm sorry I offended you – I didn't mean to imply that you were at fault." Conversational repair requires emotional intelligence to recognize that a problem has occurred and know how to fix it.

While interpersonal communication styles can easily influence respect and other aspects of procedural justice, organizational research has found that verbal and nonverbal communication can be easily misunderstood or distorted, and can even contradict each other (Clampitt, 1991; Vasu et al., 1998). This communication breakdown can have serious consequences for these encounters. Sometimes the words used by the sender can mean something different to the receiver. Body-worn camera data and survey data can help us determine if and when miscommunication occurs.

Also, nonverbal communication can send a message or attitude (Bolton, 1985; Leathers, 1992), such as when arms are folded across the chest, facial frowning or head shaking, eyes rolling, or conversely, smiling, eye contact, positive tone of voice, and head nodding. Whether it is facial expressions or body language or tone of voice, the person is sending a message. Again, all of this remains unmeasured at this point.

Over many years, Paul Ekman and Wallace Friesen created a taxonomy of facial expressions, finding forty-three distinct muscular movements (Gladwell, 2005). The basic point here is that our face can express our emotions, whether it be anger, fear, sadness, surprise, disgust, happiness, or other emotions. During police-public contacts, if officers become better at quickly identifying and understanding emotional expressions, they can strengthen their communication skills and manage their own emotions. Of course, we need to reliably measure some of these facial expressions and how they are interpreted before police training.

5.1.2 Voice

The second core principle of procedural justice is voice. Whether you look at feminist theory (e.g., Abrams, 1999) or personal efficacy research in psychology (Bandura, 1997, 2006), you will see that human beings seek to be autonomous agents who are self-governing and self-efficacious. In other words, we want to be in control of ourselves (make decisions on our own) and be in control of our immediate environment. In fact, those who feel efficacious are more likely to achieve their goals (Meichenbaum, 1984; Schunk & Zimmerman, 1994). Supporting this work, social psychological research on Brehm's reactance theory indicates that people will react negatively against threats to their individual freedom to make decisions (Brehm & Brehm, 2013; The Decision Lab, 2024).

Listening skills are essential for effective communication and for giving voice to others, but most of us are poor listeners. Too often, we are waiting for our chance to talk and even interrupt the person talking to make our point or take some action. As Vasu and colleagues note (1998), the literature distinguishes between the "deliberative listener" who is listening for information, and the "active listener" who is seeking to understand the person and their feelings. We should do both. The latter is where empathy comes in. Officers must be motivated to listen for both information and feelings, and when doing so, avoid passing judgment regarding the individual without all the facts.

Officers, like all of us, must learn how to have "difficult conversations" (Stone et al., 2023). Experts have offered strategies for having such conversations in a way that causes less stress and helps to resolve interpersonal differences and reach positive outcomes. These strategies include controlling your emotions and not being defensive when being attacked or accused of something, and listening carefully to the message that is being communicated behind the words. For example, officers should keep their cool when someone is angry about receiving a ticket ("Why are you wasting your time stopping me for no reason?") or blames the officer for a negative experience ("What took you so long to get here?").

All of this work should be taken into consideration as we seek to minimize any unnecessary, nonnegotiable commands by police officers to civilians. Officers must be careful that their actions do not suppress this human desire for agency and control unless absolutely necessary. Police are trained to believe they have the ultimate authority to enforce the law, and thus, civilians who challenge that authority are not always well received. Hence, new measures should capture whether officers engaged in active listening (i.e., giving voice) during the interaction, even when they receive negative information.

5.1.3 Neutrality

The perception of police neutrality is absolutely essential for gaining legitimacy, as the public today is very sensitive to any type of police bias. Eck and Rosenbaum (1994) posited that the public evaluates police performance using "three Es" – effectiveness, efficiency, and equity. Somehow, equity has been largely ignored as a defining feature of evidence-based policing.

Consent decrees have investigated a range of unconstitutional policing practices in American cities that pertain to police neutrality, including bias in use of force, stops, searches, and arrests, as well as racist and sexist language (e.g., see D'Souza et al., 2019). Today, the LGBTQ+ community, religious communities, and mental health communities, for example, have grown increasingly concerned about mistreatment by the police. Thus, the time has come to better measure the public's experience with the police, including these vulnerable groups. For example, as noted in Section 3.1, not only do police show bias in traffic stops and searches but also people of color are more fearful, resentful, and humiliated by these encounters, and feel discriminated against.

I should note that neutrality is closely linked to other elements in the procedural justice model. In other words, recipients of police service are less likely to feel that the police are being discriminatory or unfair if they feel they have a voice in the process, feel they are treated with dignity and respect, and feel the officer was genuinely concerned for their welfare (Skogan & Frydl, 2004).

5.1.4 Trustworthiness through Empathy

Police trustworthiness is the fourth key component of procedural justice. Our research on police contacts in fifty-three large cities has identified a core communication skill that is linked to voice and trustworthiness, namely, empathy (Rosenbaum et al., 2017). As we describe it, "[p]eople respond positively when others can understand their point of view, feelings, and circumstances, and respond with compassion, reassurance, and comfort rather than indifference, criticism, or blaming" (p.115).

Empathy can be viewed as a three-step psychological process (Kanov et al., 2004): (1) noticing that the other person is suffering; (2) feeling their experience by imagining their pain; and (3) responding or acting to ease or eliminate their suffering. Beyond feelings, empathy involves cognition. Various studies on "perspective taking" and "emotional intelligence" describe a cognitive skill set that allows you to recognize other people's mental states, recognize the hidden meaning behind what they are saying, anticipate their actions, be aware of your own emotions, and be aware of your own impact on someone. Researchers have mapped out multiple developmental stages of perspective taking (Elfers et al., 2008). Thus, social dynamics can get very complicated, but they are important for understanding interpersonal communication. Perspective taking is part of the empathy process and has shown benefits. For example, several experiments have shown that perspective taking can prevent automatic racial bias (Todd et al., 2011). Other experiments have shown that empathy traits can lead to more prosocial helping behavior (Xiao et al., 2021).

The third component of compassionate communication involves responding. The police need to go beyond noticing and feeling to doing something. Showing compassion requires action, such as emotional support, advice, or practical assistance. This means doing whatever you can do (given your time, resources, and skill) to alleviate the person's pain or suffering. This might include both nonverbal responses (e.g., nodding your head in agreement, facial expressions, body orientation, or simply showing up on time) and verbal responses (e.g., expressing sympathy and providing advice), but remaining neutral and objective as a professional.

Clearly, empathy and perspective taking stem from emotional intelligence. Officers will benefit greatly from being able to determine how their empathetic (nor nonempathetic) behavior has affected the person with whom they are interacting. Empathy is extremely important when responding to victims of personal and property crime, as they care deeply about how they are treated by the police (Elliott et al., 2012). Too often, victims of violence in the United States experience negative, unsupportive reactions from professionals. Sexual assault victims in particular receive a range of negative responses (Ullman, 2000), including police failure to properly investigate (Southall, 2022), which have been shown to inhibit their psychological recovery and reduce the likelihood of future disclosure or reporting to authorities (Ahrens, 2006; Lorenz, 2017; Starzynski et al., 2005; Ullman, 1999). For example, millions of rape kits used to test for DNA have gone untested in the United States because of doubts about the victim's report (Nadolny et al., 2024), leaving offenders on the streets and victims upset. In England and Wales, of the nearly 2,000 victims of rape and sexual assault surveyed in the first half of 2023, "75% of respondents said their mental health had worsened as a result of their police experience, 55% of respondents said their physical health decreased, 54% said their trust in police declined" (Hohl et al., 2024, p. 45). Many survivors did not feel their reports were taken seriously by the police. They felt they were not listened to, were blamed for what happened, and were not treated with kindness and understanding. As a result, many expressed unwillingness to report future sexual offenses. In 2022, charges were brought in only 2.1 percent of all reported rape cases in England and Wales (Hohl & Stanko, 2024). Thus, the link between procedural justice and future offending is very clear.

Related to trustworthiness and empathy is the importance of police providing explanations for their decisions and actions. Victims and bystanders want to know why the police are asking certain questions, making certain demands, or making certain decisions. To show empathy and compassion, police will need to slow down, listen to people's anger, fears, and concerns, and answer their questions. Too often police feel they need to run from call to call and do not have time to "chat" with anyone, which is simply not true in most cities. Thus, another communication skill in short supply is patience.

5.2 Summary of Potential New Measures

In sum, police-public encounters are much more complex than suggested by enforcement statistics on traffic citations, arrests, and use of force. Procedural justice is a defining feature of police-public interactions. The officer's respectfulness, fairness and impartiality, emotional and informational support, and other communication skills will determine whether community residents are satisfied with their encounter, will work with the police in the future, and will obey the law themselves. Therefore, procedural justice should be measured and used by police agencies in a manner that will increase both police legitimacy and public safety.

6 Building and Testing New Systems of Measurement

In support of translational criminology, this Element seeks to develop strategies that move us from "evidence to action" (La Vigne, 2024) – strategies that lead to real change in police organizations. The time has come to build and test new systems of measurement to enhance procedural justice during police-public encounters, and thus create police organizations that employ what Rahr & Rice (2015) call "guardians" rather than "warriors." My proposal springs from a basic principle of organizational management: If you measure something, you can manage it and hold employees accountable for achieving it. Conversely, if you fail to measure something, then management is sending the message to employees that it doesn't matter and officers can ignore it as they go about their work. Thus, the time has come to "measure what matters to the public" – procedural justice – and build these data into new management systems. Two new data systems are proposed here: contact surveys and BWCs.

6.1 Contact Surveys

For many years policing scholars have been promoting community surveys as a method of evaluating public satisfaction with the police (e.g., Brown & Benedict, 2002; Decker, 1981; Fridell & Wycoff, 2004), and now such surveys are widely employed. However, there are several major limitations to previous and ongoing community surveys: (1) the findings cannot be disaggregated to small geographic areas – they are typically citywide or national, (2) they are one-time "snapshots" of community perceptions, not ongoing data collection systems, (3) they cannot be linked to officer performance evaluations or accountability systems, and (4) they only capture the general public's perceptions of the police, which, as others have pointed out, tends to be "stereotypical views about law enforcement rather than lived experiences" (Carmichael et al., 2021, p. 99). To be clear, results from the national Police-Public Contact Survey indicate that only 21 percent of Americans have contact with the police in a given year (Tapp & Davis, 2022). In other words, eight out of ten community survey respondents have no "lived experience" with the police. Hence, the time has come to give voice to the one in five Americans who have experiential knowledge of actual police behavior.

The Police-Public Contact Survey introduced by the Bureau of Justice Statistics is a good start, but this is a national survey that is only administered every few years, and only asks community members about police contacts within the last year. As the President's Task Force (2015) noted, "these surveys do not reflect what is happening every day at the local level when police interact with members of the communities they serve" (p. 24). Clearly, we need to capture the public's experience quickly – within the first week or two – not a year later. Research indicates that the passage of time has an adverse effect on human recall (Baddeley et al., 2009; Barrouillet & Camos, 2012). Memory will simply decay over time and can be biased by what researchers call "retroactive interference," where new information interferes with the mental retrieval of old information.

The direct benefits of an ongoing Contact Survey Program are numerous. First, community members who are stopped by the police or call the police for help will be given a voice and empowered in a relationship that has, historically, been perceived as one-sided. This measurement system will also incentivize a new definition of good policing, encouraging the police to "serve and protect" in a procedurally just manner. The contact survey data will help police agencies identify specific skills and circumstances where programmatic intervention will strengthen procedural justice during police-public encounters.

6.1.1 Contact Survey Content and Methods

Contact surveys need to be institutionalized at the local level, as a few small cities are beginning to do now (see Davies, 2022), but with methods and measures that meet social science standards and can be integrated into a national system of data collection. We learned a great deal from introducing a contact survey in fifty-three large cities as part of the National Police Research Platform (Rosenbaum et al., 2017), funded by the National Institute of Justice. Similar to the platform project, I would recommend that the proposed contact survey and associated methodologies be the result of meetings with a small group of community leaders, police chiefs/sheriffs, AI experts, and policing scholars with knowledge of procedural justice research. To maximize response rates, I would recommend a relatively short survey, that is, no more than fifteen to twenty questions.

We asked police chiefs to mail letters to community members who have had a recent police contact (i.e., in the past two weeks), but mailing letters is a time-consuming and expensive approach. Now, I would propose that officers be required to distribute business cards with a survey invitation and QR code that provides a link to the survey, to be completed either online or by telephone (we did both successfully). Importantly, an independent agency will need to follow up with text messages to ensure a reasonable response rate. Finally, the city will need a public education campaign, using social media, billboards, and flyers, to make the community aware of this new program and encourage their participation.

Based on the research cited above, I have suggested several relevant topics for the survey in the Online Appendix. Procedural justice should be the main focus, but consideration should be given to related topics, such as threats and use of force, de-escalation, empathy/compassion, social etiquette, willingness to work with the police, trust in the police, and overall satisfaction with the experience.

6.1.2 Linking the Survey Data to Other Agency Data

To avoid a lengthy survey and to provide more context about the incident, the police records division will need to routinely download certain data elements connected with police reports and create a separate database that can be linked to the survey responses. These data elements would include the incident number, demographic information, and other information needed for analysis (see Section 7.1.1).

6.2 Body-Worn Cameras

I envision BWC data as a major source of police reforms in the future, but BWC data have yet to be used for meaningful organizational changes. Here I am proposing that such data be used for measuring the quality of police services and changing incentive structures. For example, when BWC footage of police stops from one California agency was hand-coded using words spoken, the authors found that officers used less respectful language when talking to people of color than when talking to white drivers (Voigt et al., 2017). From this work, we can begin to see the richness and value of BWC data. However, the hand-coding of BWC data by human beings is far too time-consuming and, therefore, must be replaced by BWC data analytics to have widespread utility.

Today, software built with artificial intelligence (AI) is now being developed and field tested, so that cities can engage in more systematic and proactive reviews of police-community interactions captured with BWCs (e.g., Farooq, 2024; Polis Solutions, 2024). The most significant project to date is what I will call "the Dallas Project." Funded by the National Institute of Justice, this project involved a collaboration between the National Policing Institute, Polis Solutions, the Caruth Policing Institute at the University of North Texas at Dallas, and the Dallas Police Department (Dolly et al., 2024). This initiative was able to field test software developed by Polis Solutions called TrustStat to "analyze verbal and non-verbal cues from BWC footage, identifying behaviors aligned with procedural justice principles." Human coders were trained to rate the same videos to assess the degree of correspondence between AI and human perceptions of procedural justice during these police-public encounters. The results indicate a high degree of correlation, suggesting that AI software has strong potential to help us understand the interpersonal dynamics that occur during a vast array of police-public encounters that currently go unmeasured.

This opens the door for police agencies to look far beyond the anecdotal investigations of a few "bad officers" and identify patterns of behavior for all officers. Of course, the Dallas project has limitations, as acknowledged by the authors. The sample of videos was limited to those from the Dallas Police Department and did not include force incidents. Second, the sample of human coders was limited to a handful of community members, university faculty, and police personnel from Dallas. Finally, and most importantly, the project did not collect data from those individuals who interacted with the officers in these videos to gain their perceptions of what transpired and their views of procedural justice. As the authors note, "[w]hat may seem like a procedurally just interaction may be objectionable or offensive to the community member experiencing it." Thus, while the Dallas project is extremely important and promising, more work is needed to refine the measures, test external validity with a diversity of videos and coders, and connect AI results with contact survey data.

6.3 Analysis of New Data

Beginning with BWC data, we need to deconstruct and categorize what is being communicated and how it is being communicated both verbally and nonverbally. For example, did the officers introduce themselves and ask relevant questions? Did they listen carefully without interrupting? How often did they use commanding or demeaning language, raise their voice, show anger, seem rushed, indifferent, impatient, or blame the civilian for what happened? How often did they show patience, speak in a soft tone, show kindness, respect, empathy, and concern for the person's welfare? How often did they answer questions, offer individual guidance, or provide information about services? Nonverbally, did the officer use their head, face, or arms to communicate support, indifference, or negativity?

While the BWC data will be more extensive than the contact survey data, they should overlap on key dimensions of procedural justice to allow testing for convergent validity. Also, we can expect that combining these complementary datasets for the same incidents will allow researchers to make significant advances in our knowledge of the antecedents and consequences of procedural justice. When one dataset suggests a pattern, the other dataset can be used to provide new insights or explanations. For example, when an officer uses specific language (based on BWC data), does it influence the community members' perceptions of that officer and level of procedural justice (based on contact survey data)?

Conversational analysis can look at the tone, pitch, intonation, and interruptions that occur in conversations (e.g., Shon, 2024), and this can be captured with sophisticated AI analysis of BWC data. Since 2017, when Google created the "transformer" architecture for language translation, we have witnessed a revolution in AI technology (Toews, 2023), leading to generative AI like ChatGPT. We now have superfast semiconductors that are beginning to solve many of society's problems (60 minutes, 2024). For the current proposal, thousands of words and behaviors can now be analyzed in seconds by AI to identify patterns and extract meaning. How these words are received and interpreted by community members will require a contact survey that can inform these AI algorithms.

Applications of AI in the policing field can build upon the impressive use of AI to evaluate physical- and mental health-related interventions and provide feedback to improve diagnosis, treatment, and bedside manners (Bedmutha et al., 2024; Bickman et al., 2016; Love-Koh, et al., 2018; Ryan et al., 2019). Ryan and colleagues (2019) describe how AI could be used to measure the meaning of words, turn taking, and the tone and style of communication.

For policing, the analysis of BWC recordings and contact survey data should eventually produce a reliable PJ Index and independent subcomponents that determine the level of procedural justice and related communication skills exhibited by police officers during their encounters. Subindexes within the overall PJ Index might include voice, respect, fairness, emotional control, empathy, and perhaps other dimensions such as general competence. Once we have established reliable and valid indicators of procedural-justice-related behaviors, we can begin to examine their relationship to specific outcomes, as shown in Figure 3. For example, is disrespect by the officer a stronger predictor of civilian resistance than lack of empathy by the officer?

However, reality is more complex, as reflected in Figure 4. Interpersonal communication can be extremely complex, so we need to expand our chart here

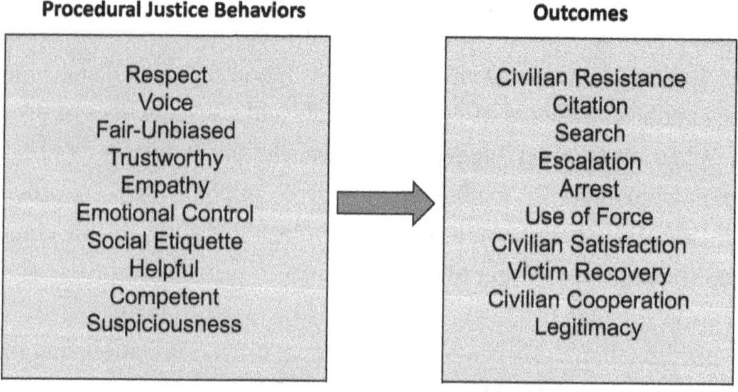

Figure 3 Linking behaviors and outcomes.

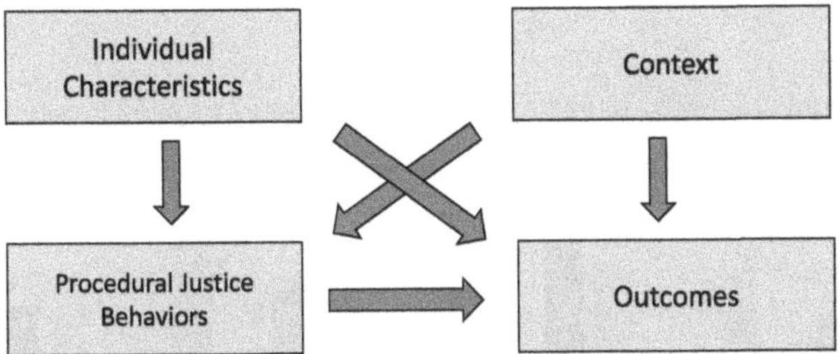

Figure 4 The complexity of interpersonal communication: AI and BWC data.

to consider both the *context* in which the encounter occurred and the *demographics* of the participants. We need to consider the individual characteristics of *both* the officer and the civilian involved – their race, age, ethnicity, gender identity, sexual orientation, disability, language proficiency, and other characteristics. I expect that AI analysis of BWC data will allow us to identify a large set of characteristics and behaviors that can be linked to procedural justice, and some of these perceptions and actions may be driven by prejudice and stereotypes.

As one example of *demographic* effects, we collected procedural justice data through a contact survey in Chicago. With the help of Jon Maskaly, I looked at three demographic characteristics (age, race/ethnicity, and gender identity) of 3,646 people who were stopped by the Chicago police in 2014 and 2015, and matched them with the characteristics of the officers who stopped them. I hypothesized that the more matching that occurred between the demographics of the officer and the community member, the higher the procedural justice scores assigned to the officer. The results support this matching hypothesis. As shown in Figure 5, as the number of demographic matches increased (0, 1, 2, 3), community members reported more satisfaction with the encounter, more trust of the officer, more respect from the officer, and perceived less officer bias against them.

However, not all matches are the same. Female-female matches outperformed male-male matches across multiple dimensions of procedural justice. My guess is that too much testosterone is at work when the males are paired. Male officers are more inclined to experience the "masculinity threat" (Richardson & Goff, 2014), and therefore feel the need to response with authority to restore their status as the "Alpha male."

No doubt, reality is even more complex than these findings suggest. The lower procedural justice scores that result from age mismatches in general could be due to many factors. For example, the use of certain words might be miscommunicated across different generations (Twenge, 2023). Using slang,

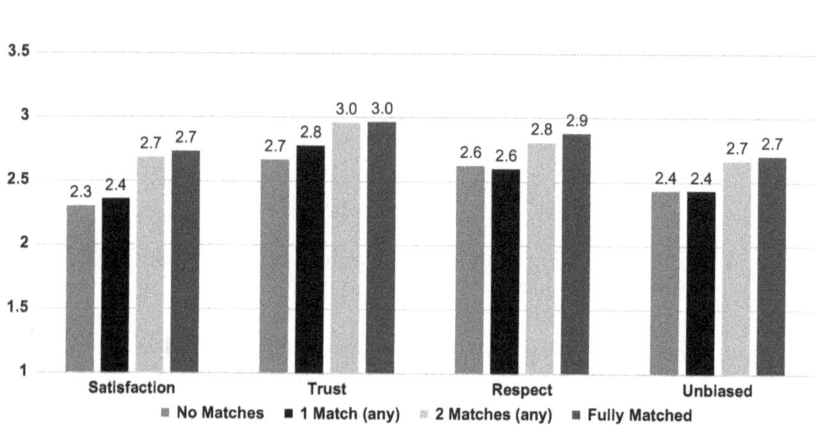

Figure 5 Procedural justice scores by number of civilian/officer demographic matches on age, race, gender.

a Gen X civilian (born 1965–79) might say to new Gen Z officer (born 1995–2012), "You seem like a headbanger." The younger officer might respond defensively, "I would never harm anyone unless they deserved it," not realizing the older civilian is referring to heavy metal music lovers.

In terms of *context*, there are many variables to consider. For example, what is the level of poverty in the neighborhood where the interaction occurred? What is the level of crime and disorder? Did the encounter occur in a hot spot of crime? Are the police responding to a domestic violence incident or making a traffic stop? How long did the encounter last?

In the future, after extensive training with large datasets, AI should be able to distinguish between individual officers in their style of communication and interaction with other people, indicating levels of emotional intelligence, procedural justice, empathy, and other interpersonal skills that are more or less effective in building trust with different types of community members. For example, imagine that Officer A does much better when interacting with younger people than with older people. Officer B does well with most groups, except when someone questions his authority, and then his ego is quickly bruised and he tends to threaten the person with punishment. Officer C receives high procedural justice scores in general, except when entering a crime hot spot, where he quickly becomes an aggressive warrior who is suspicious of everyone he encounters.

The specific communication skills that lead to these outcomes should be determined. Some actions or words may cause tensions to escalate and even result in use of force or other enforcement actions, while other actions lead to de-escalation. In addition, we need to look at how various police behaviors are perceived by the community members in different settings. Some actions may have little impact, while others produce negative sentiment and perceived injustice.

Thus, our knowledge should expand exponentially with the analysis of new data from BWCs and contact surveys, and this information can be used to help officers adjust to different settings and different civilians. The number of statistical interactions between personal and contextual variables could be very large and very helpful. Beyond individual officers, we will learn which procedural justice behaviors are the strongest predictors of outcomes in general, and therefore should be given more attention throughout the organization.

6.3.1 Hot Spots of Procedural Injustice and Hot Individuals

These analyses may identify what I will call "hot spots of procedural injustice," that is, small geographic areas where procedural injustice by the police is higher than surrounding areas. Many years ago I recommended the use of surveys to study small geographic areas (Rosenbaum & Lavrakas, 1995). With large enough samples, the contact survey dataset should generate new research findings on the factors that contribute to hot spots of procedural injustice, which, in turn, could advance our understanding of geo-based crime patterns. We know that police-community relations are especially strained in low-income neighborhoods of color, where hot spots of crime are more likely to occur, but we have yet to determine whether there is variability in procedural justice within or between these areas, and if so, what are the causes and effects. What is the degree and conditions of overlap between hot spots of crime and hot spots of procedural injustice? The police should have more success in solving crime if they have a procedurally just relationship with community members who frequent hot spots.

Beyond geography, these new datasets should be used to identify "hot officers" and "hot civilians." To begin with, each officer should have their own PJ Index and subindex scores that can be compared to other officers. Hot officers could be defined as those officers whose PJ scores are at least two standard deviations *below* the mean for all officers serving in similar situations. This information should remain confidential but can be used for training and coaching. Hot civilians could be defined as community members whose behavior involves the initiation of, or negative response to, procedural injustice during interactions with the police (e.g., disrespectful language or noncompliance). Understanding these patterns is important. In other words, what specific behaviors by civilians cause what specific types of officers to engage in what specific types of procedural injustice? Here too, these findings can be used to train all officers in how to recognize these general patterns and respond appropriately.

We must also be able to analyze the data to identify "Exemplary Officers," defined as those officers whose PJ Index scores are at least two standard deviations *above* the mean for all officers serving in similar situations. We must acknowledge and reward their exceptional performance and use it as a model for other officers to follow.

Finally, the analysis should produce aggregate PJ Index scores as the foundation for organizational change. Procedural Justice Indexes should be generated for all supervisors (i.e., the average of all scores for employees who report to them), thus allowing the identification of hot supervisors and exemplary supervisors. In addition, PJ Indexes should also be calculated for the city as a whole, police districts, beats, shifts, and special units, for internal changes discussed in Section 7. Finally, given the widespread concern about explicit or implicit police bias, the analysis should, to the extent possible, include breakdowns by constitutionally protected classes of service recipients.

6.4 Measurement Conclusion

The collection and analysis of new procedural justice data from BWCs and contact surveys is the first large step in changing police culture and service, but it is only the beginning. We must be able to translate these data patterns into evidence-based policing that results in significant improvements in police-public interactions.

As a psychologist, I cannot emphasize enough that human behavior is shaped by incentives and disincentives. Today, police officers are expected to be good public servants, but there are no systems in place to support and reward such behavior. The crime-fighting behavior of "warriors" is rewarded more than the helpful and respectful behavior of "guardians." Typically, officers are rewarded for increased productivity and aggressiveness in terms of the number of citations written, arrests made, guns and drugs recovered, and crimes investigated, not the manner in which community members are treated. Many police agencies still have informal quotas for the number of stops or tickets written in a given time period, regardless of the justification for enforcement (Fielding, 2022; Ossei-Owusu, 2016), although many laws now prohibit such practices because they can result in racial profiling.

Police officers themselves would agree with my critique of current reward structures. Our national survey found that only one-third of the officers felt that "employees who consistently do a good job are rewarded," and two-thirds felt that "the department is more interested in measuring activity than the quality of work" (see Cordner, 2017). If we care about the quality of police work, then the time has come to change the structure of incentives and accountability.

7 Using Data to Change Modern Policing

The collection, analysis, and reporting of new performance data is a waste of time if a system is not created for police organizations to *use these data* for management purposes. The entire chain of command will need to be involved in this process. I am proposing a coordinated approach that involves both internal and external strategies of reform. Here, I will provide a brief summary of the changes needed to alter street-level behavior, with a focus on new data collection, accountability, and performance evaluation systems. Without proper incentive structures, management will continue to face a crisis of public confidence and will be unable to monitor or shape the performance of its officers on the street.

7.1 External Changes

7.1.1 Police Performance Agency (PPA) and Community Involvement

Police agencies have repeatedly experienced difficulty introducing and sustaining major organizational reforms and being objective in self-assessment. Hence, the new data systems should be managed by a unit of government that is completely independent of the police department to gain public trust, protect confidentiality, and ensure strong implementation of the data collection system. Let's call this the Police Performance Agency (PPA). The PPA, working closely with community leaders, police personnel, a survey laboratory, and a company specializing in using AI to analyze BWC data, would have the primary responsibility for overseeing the collection, analysis, and reporting of findings. The PPA would oversee the work of a survey laboratory involving contact survey data and the work of an AI company involving BWC data. Dashboards for police management would be created. The PPA would also work with an audit unit within the police agency to ensure that all employees, from police officers to managers, are following new policies regarding this system and using data dashboards properly. The PPA must also conduct an ongoing audit to ensure that officers are distributing contact survey business cards for all targeted incidents involving a police report, and not simply handing them out selectively after positive encounters. Telephone calls, text messages, or emails can be used to contact potential survey respondents to ask whether they were handed a business card by the officer.

The community has a very important role as a contact survey respondent, providing information about the quality of their recent contact with the police.

They can also assist the PPA in creating a public awareness campaign to inform the community of the contact survey program, its importance, and how community members can participate with their identity protected. Finally, certain community members should be invited to participate in police training to share their lived experience, which can help to create empathy and understanding among officers.

To create the dashboards with the relevant breakdowns, the PPA would need to receive a database from the department's record management division with information about the police-public contacts being analyzed, for example, incident number, date, characteristics of the incident (traffic stop, traffic accident, or crime incident), unit and supervisor involved, any action taken (search, warning, citation, arrest, and/or use of force), the location (precinct, district, beat, and block), time of day, and the demographics of both the community member and officer involved (race/ethnicity, age, gender, unit, etc.). Some agencies have created good "Metadata" for BWC systems (White et al., 2023) that include some of these data points and more, such as the exact location and length of the encounter. These "tags" will also be needed for the survey dataset. After protecting the identity of the community member and the officer, these downloads should be provided to the independent agency on a monthly basis to allow for the generation of reports on PJ Index performance.

The full database will serve as the basis for reports and feedback regarding specific precincts, districts, units, supervisors, and individual officers. Importantly, the use of police records and metadata not only provides the context for examining different patterns of procedural justice but also helps to keep the contact survey very short (i.e., without demographic or incident information), thus increasing community response rates.

Also, community feedback and education should be one by-product of this new measurement system. Frankly, the escalation of tension or negative sentiment during police-public encounters can be the result of actions taken by the police officer *and/or* the community member. Data from the BWCs and contact surveys could teach us a great deal about the behavior patterns of community members as well as officers, and the dynamics of this exchange. Similar to the analysis of police behavior, this information on civilian behavior should be used to educate the general public and police officers about ways they might be able to prevent the escalation of conflict and remain safe.

7.2 Internal Changes

To improve the quality of police services and police legitimacy, the new measurement system must be translated into organizational changes that are focused on improving officers' communication skills and management accountability for these skills. Other policing scholars have also been critical of past changes and have suggested a variety of evidence-based organizational changes to make policing more effective (Lum, 2021; Lum & Nagin, 2017; Skolnick & Fyfe, 1993). The focus here is on how two new data systems can be used to change police culture and strengthen procedural justice during routine encounters with the public. The key to successful reform is to change performance evaluations and accountability systems for personnel at all levels of the organization. Here I briefly describe some of these evidence-based changes that can help advance the science of performance measurement and evaluation, and thus help agencies become "learning laboratories" (Maguire, 2004b).

7.2.1 Performance Evaluations

Performance evaluation systems should be completely redesigned. New dashboards should be built using data from contact surveys and BWCs. While some traditional metrics should be retained (e.g., internal and external complaints), special attention should be given to the quality of service delivered and procedural justice.

Procedural Justice Index scores, computed outside the agency, should be used thoughtfully by supervisors to evaluate individual officers. For decades, agencies have recorded officer-level data on many variables, including the number of stops, citations, arrests, force applications, and citizen complaints, so there is no compelling reason why they cannot retain and use data on the quality of service delivered and procedural justice in particular.

7.2.2 Supervision with Good Data

Anyone who studies police organizations understands that first-line supervisors play a critical role in organizational change – they communicate the norms and values of management, administer rewards and punishments, and protect their employees from harm (Van Maanen, 1983). Organizational research in different settings has taught us that supervisors need to communicate effectively with their employees to create effective working conditions and job satisfaction (Katz & Kahn, 1966; Pincus, 1986). This holds true for police organizations as well.

In the present context, police supervisors should be required to use the new dashboard data on procedural justice to identify at-risk employees as well as exemplary employees. I see enormous potential for EIS in the future, as they represent a proactive, data-driven system to examine behavioral patterns and predict the performance of individual officers (Walker & Milligan, 2006;

Walker et al., 2000). Of course, criminologists love to predict human behavior, as the entire field of criminology was built on successfully predicting delinquency and geographic crime patterns.

Using reliable and valid PJ Indexes, supervisors should identify and intervene with those individuals who score significantly above or below the mean of comparable officers. For consistently high-scoring officers, their supervisor should acknowledge such achievement with verbal praise, and consider certificates, awards, and pay raises. For consistently low-scoring officers, supervisors need to intervene with additional supervision, coaching, and training. Again, I want to remind police administrators that rewarding desired behaviors and discouraging undesirable behaviors is the basic process by which behavior change is achieved, and it needs to occur frequently. Hence, the typical annual performance evaluation should be supplemented by more frequent observations and meetings with officers who will benefit from assistance or praise.

Police organizations that follow procedural justice principles (what I call "Organizational Justice") can increase job satisfaction and rule compliance among their employees (Rosenbaum & McCarty, 2017). Also, research indicates that when supervisors talk through a recent officer-civilian encounter using procedural justice principles, they can reduce incidents of arrest and use of force (Owens et al., 2015).

7.2.3 Accountability Unit and Meetings

Building on the CompStat model, police departments should hold regular meetings, where a powerful, internal accountability unit and senior management share statistics on procedural justice with all command personnel. I have called them "RespectStat meetings" (McCarthy & Rosenbaum, 2015), but the name is not important. As suggested earlier, data from the contact survey and BWC systems should produce quantitative scores on the PJ Index and subindexes for each precinct/district, shift, unit, types of incident/call, demographics of the officer, and demographics of the community member. The results will likely indicate differences in performance across these variables, begging the question of what is contributing to these differences and what can be done to enhance performance in certain areas. These accountability meetings should put immediate pressure on commanders and supervisors to increase their scores before the next meeting.

Leaders should create a problem-solving culture to aid in this process. Using a problem-oriented policing (POP) framework with the SARA model, managers should be taught to identify specific patterns and problems in procedural justice performance. Then, they must be taught to propose, implement, and evaluate new methods for improving officers' performance on these indicators.

Commanders and middle managers should encourage this type of problem-solving with brainstorming sessions. De-policing that reduces public safety should not be allowed as an acceptable solution.

Everyone from first-line supervisors to the Chief of Police should have certain performance standards or goals built into a strategic plan for their procedural justice program. When they achieve those goals (e.g., 80 percent of the officers under their supervision achieved PJ Index scores above a certain level), these supervisors should be acknowledged and rewarded in some way.

I was impressed with the MAX program (Management Analytics for Excellence) that was introduced in the New Orleans Police Department in 2016 (Morgan et al., 2017). Using dashboards, visual maps, report cards, and monthly meetings, MAX sought to hold administrators accountable for changes in specific performance metrics relevant to the consent decree. Like CompStat, they held monthly MAX meetings, but unlike CompStat, the metrics reach far beyond crime statistics to include data on stops, searches, use of force, and even procedural justice. The role of supervisors was given special attention. For procedural justice, every month two team members reviewed BWC footage from seven police stops in each district and scored the officer (yes or no) on several dimensions, such as whether they introduced themselves, explained their actions, and listened to the subject. When searches and use of force are involved, the reviewers also judge whether officers were "reasonably professional and courteous."

The MAX system represents a significant change in police accountability, requiring that managers do something to improve metrics other than crime and enforcement statistics. In New Orleans, scores improved quickly, presumably because of monthly downward pressure in the chain of command to move from "Red" to "Green" before the next meeting. However, given that the entire process is internally controlled under pressure from a consent monitor, the process of change (e.g., feedback to individual officers) and the validity of the metrics remain uncertain. Also, the small samples of BWC footage will not be representative of the department overall or even the few individuals selected. The scoring system is also unlikely to meet scientific standards of reliability. Nevertheless, this a laudable first initiative.

Clearly, if the MAX system were able to use AI to analyze BWC footage, that would dramatically reduce the workload of reviewers and improve the reliability and validity of these accountability metrics. Furthermore, adding contact survey data to this process would be a significant enhancement of this data-driven approach. We encourage law enforcement agencies to draw on this framework to build a new service-oriented accountability system using new procedural justice data from contact surveys and BWCs that is analyzed with sophisticated AI algorithms.

This type of accountability system should reach beyond commanders to mid-level managers and front-line supervisors. Supervisors should be given training and coaching on how to interpret and use the PJ Indexes to enhance officers' performance on the job. However, the agency must exercise caution when comparing officers or supervisors who are assigned to precincts or shifts with vastly different levels of crime and poverty. At a minimum, organizational units should be compared against themselves and should be expected to show improvement in their scores over time.

With enough data, sophisticated breakdowns of the data are likely to reveal interesting patterns that deserve attention. Specific patterns could be discussed at these department-wide meetings if they occur above the individual level to protect confidentiality. Imagine, for example, that an agency is having a problem with low PJ Index scores with *detectives*, but only those working the *evening shift* and only when interviewing *sexual assault victims* and only when they show a *lack of empathy*. Or perhaps there is a PJ Index problem in District 5, but only for *Patrol Officers* who are using *disrespectful language*, but only during *traffic stops* and only with drivers *under twenty-five years of age*. Handed these findings, the job of management is to engage in problem-solving sessions where the SARA model is used to fully understand the nature of the problem and respond appropriately. This might include additional coaching, training and supervision, or even reassignments to provide additional support. Managers at all levels should be expected to discuss actions taken and progress made on PJ Indexes at future PJ meetings.

If enough procedural justice data is collected, it can be used to assess variability across small geographic areas. Just as criminologists have identified hot spots of crime, we should be able to identify hot spots of procedural injustice. As noted earlier, given the overrepresentation of minorities near hot spots of crime, and given the tendency of officers to respond more aggressively in areas where they hold prejudicial suspicions of criminality, there is a good chance that PJ Index scores will be lower in these areas. District commanders and other supervisors should be made aware of these hot spots of procedural injustice and use the SARA model as part of their brainstorming sessions.

Hence, this new data system should lead to a reduction in the number of procedural injustice hot spots, which in turn should lead to greater trust in, and cooperation with, the police. This cooperation should help to reduce hot spots of crime. However, agencies may also discover hot spots of procedural injustice that are outside the hot spots of crime. These micro places should be addressed as well, as they might contribute to legal cynicism and increase the chances that additional hot spots of crime will emerge.

Agencies should continue accountability for crime reduction, but should focus more on the prevention of crime than on reactive enforcement, especially strategies that engage the community to build public trust. For example, the Portland Police Bureau in Oregon has developed an app that allows officers to keep track of all public meetings they attend and the number of people in attendance.

Other individual-level performance metrics can be included in accountability meetings, such the number of internal and external complaints against officers, applications of force, sick days taken, and poorly written police reports, to give a few examples (for a sophisticated look at force applications, see Jonathan-Zamir et al., 2024). Again, means and standard deviations should be calculated with appropriate comparisons. My point here is that procedural justice is not meant to replace all other forms of accountability.

The internal audit and evaluation unit should be responsible for working with the PPA to prepare the PJ Index scores and other data for accountability meetings. They would have other responsibilities, such as monitoring the data-driven dashboards to ensure that they are user-friendly and contain data points that are essential for high-quality supervision. They should also be responsible for the quality of data and reports that are included in the EIS program to avoid the "garbage in, garbage out" problem. The audit and evaluation unit would also audit compliance with new policies, including the proper use and activation of BWCs.

Clearly, senior management will need to introduce new incentives that value procedural justice as a central goal of the organization. The performance of mid-level managers and first-line supervisors should be evaluated based on the quality and quantity of problem-solving meetings, employee interventions that focus on improving procedural justice, and aggregate PJ Index scores of their employees. Similar to officers, managers should be rewarded for performing these tasks well and for improving procedural justice outcomes.

7.2.4 Officer Training

Training will be needed at all levels of the organization to introduce new policies and practices designed to enhance procedural justice and legitimacy, while changing the police culture. To achieve officer "buy in," officers must be reassured that this new system and training will make their job easier and safer and is designed to be supportive rather than punitive.

Lately, we see police organizations changing their policies and linking them to new training on use of force, de-escalation, and peer intervention to stop/prevent harmful behavior by other officers. This is a good start, but these trainings tend to be limited in hours, rarely involve scenario-based practice sessions, and are not evaluated to determine their effectiveness in changing street-level behavior. Furthermore, these policies and trainings tend to have a narrow focus on the misuse of force, which is a small piece of the problem. The larger problem is the police culture that negatively affects daily encounters and the image of the police, which may lead to preventable force incidents.

Trainers must address officers' skepticism about being nice to people while enforcing the law. Skeptical officers often tell me, "When I give someone a ticket, I'm never going to get a good rating." We tested that hypothesis in three cities, where we measured the officer's procedural justice or what I call "Carside Manners" *after* the officer gave the driver a ticket (Rosenbaum et al., 2015). As shown in Figure 6, there are massive differences in driver satisfaction depending on whether or not the officer treated them in a procedurally just manner. The average satisfaction score was 42 percent (dotted horizontal line). If the officer listened to the driver and was polite, the driver was about 60–62 percent satisfied with the encounter. However, when the officer did not listen and was not polite, satisfaction rating dropped to about 5–8 percent. So "Carside Manners" (procedural justice) do matter when issuing a ticket! Similarly, a randomized trial using laboratory videos by Maguire and colleagues (2023) found that procedural injustice during traffic stops works to increase anger, while procedural justice decreases anger.

As I have stated several times, we know that crime is concentrated in low-income neighborhoods where people of color and other vulnerable groups are overrepresented. History tells us that local residents often view the police as

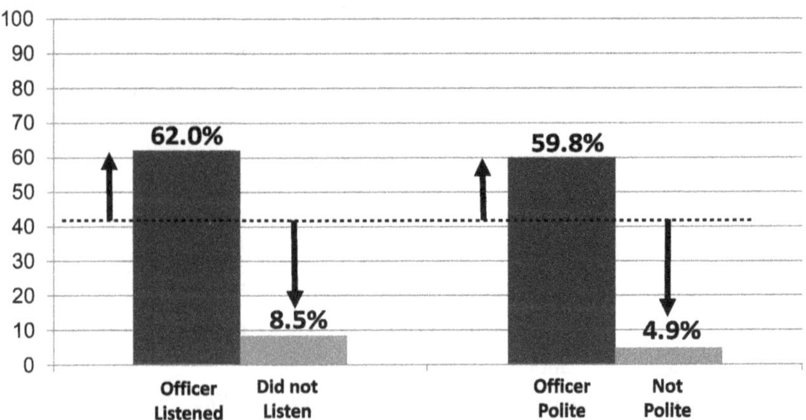

Figure 6 "Carside manners" when ticketing. (% very satisfied and somewhat satisfied).

white male intruders who are suspicious of everyone (Skolnick & Fyfe, 1993). Hence, procedural justice training and supervision will need to give special attention to issues of bias. The Black community is not the only group at risk. The prevalence of hatred and intimidation toward immigrants, Hispanics, Jews, Muslims, the homeless, and the LGBTQ+ community has become especially problematic in the United States. Again, data from the new system should be able to direct management to specific bias problems where additional training is needed and the types of interactions that need attention.

In terms of evidence-based policing, I will note that procedural justice training has shown considerable promise for improving police attitudes and behavior (Antrobus et al., 2019; Mazerolle et al., 2012; Rosenbaum & Lawrence, 2017; Sahin et al., 2017; Weisburd et al., 2022; Wheller et al., 2013; Wood et al., 2020). However, the organization must be ready for such training, otherwise you can expect a backlash. For example, while the procedural justice training for roadside checks was effective in the Australian "Queensland Community Engagement Trial" (Mazerolle et al., 2013b), the same type of training had the opposite effect in the "Scottish Community Engagement Trial" (MacQueen & Bradford, 2015) because officers were unhappy with ongoing reforms and this experiment was not well explained to them in advance (MacQueen & Bradford, 2017).

From my perspective, the most effective procedural justice training requires adult learning methods and lots of practice time with feedback sessions, similar to how officers are trained to use weapons, but more individualized. Cameras can be used to provide immediate feedback in practice sessions and to illustrate desired behaviors exhibited by exemplary officers in the field. In Chicago, we videotaped police recruits facing off with difficult role players, reviewed the recording, and then gave them feedback (Rosenbaum & Lawrence, 2017). Watching BWC footage of your own performance can also be helpful (Deck et al., 2024). Videotaped feedback has been used to enhance communication skills in various fields, from medicine (Roter et al., 2004) to martial arts (BenitezSantiago & Miltenberger, 2015). Professional athletes regularly observe videos of themselves to improve their performance. Training can also be enhanced by using virtual reality headsets to strength officers' skills (Bridges, 2024), although this work should be expanded beyond use of force decisions to building interpersonal communication skills in general, such as how to interact with victims of crime. In any event, both the quality and quantity of adult learning methods should be increased.

However, we must acknowledge the potential restrictions on building a more empathetic and emotionally intelligent workforce. Police face traumatic incidents, from dead bodies to people being shot, and this can sometimes result in post-traumatic stress disorder (PTSD), which in turn can affect brain function and decision-making (Covey et al., 2023). Long-term exposure to trauma over their career can negatively impact their physical and mental well-being (Craddock & Telesco, 2022). Also, there is the real possibility that officers, after years of exposure to intense situations and trauma, will experience "compassion fatigue," which is familiar to therapists and widespread in the healthcare industry (Cavanagh et al., 2020). Certainly, we know that some officers become hardened and cynical over time.

In the context of creating a wellness culture (and not just wellness training), agencies may be able to use instruments developed in the healthcare field to identify officers at risk of compassion fatigue, such as the Professional Quality of Life Scale or other metrics (Craddock & Telesco, 2022; Sinclair et al., 2017), and provide early intervention, such as therapy and rotating them out of high-crime, high-stress assignments.

If officers have difficulty showing empathy, they could, at a minimum, practice specific scripts or linguistic formulas to speak in an empathetic manner. In the medical field, one "bedside manners" study found that the AI language model ChatCPT was able to show significantly more "empathy" than medical doctors when answering patients' questions by using the right words (Ayers et al., 2023). Down the road, we should consider having officers interact with a chat application on the job, such as an AI chatbot, to improve their procedural justice skills appropriate for a given situation. Once we have trained AI on BWC and contact survey data, the information might be programmed into an AI chatbot wristwatch. These watches could give officers immediate feedback. For example, during the encounter, the watch might suggest (via earbuds) specific language that is responsive to the community member's actions or words. (e.g., "I'm sorry that happened to you. Can you tell me more?"). After the encounter, the watch might score the officer's procedural justice performance on different dimensions based on the words they used (e.g., "Your Respect score for this event was 9.0. Your Empathy score was only 3.0. Keep up the good work on Respect and try to improve your Empathy."). Officers should be reminded that empathy is a skill, not an unchangeable trait, and when people are reminded of this, research shows they work harder to develop it (Zaki, 2017).

7.2.5 Recruitment and Selection

After finding that "reform training" on community policing and problem-solving had limited effects, Haar (2000) noted that "[t]he best predictors of attitude change were by far the attitudes that recruits brought with them to the academy" (p. v). Taking this a step further, cities should pay more attention to the recruitment and selection of individuals who are most capable of engaging in procedurally just behaviors on the job. Given the current retention and staffing problems in law enforcement, this is a good time to stop and reflect on recruiting and hiring practices.

First, for recruitment, agencies should move away from the warrior ads with SWAT teams dropping from helicopters and begin to recruit individuals with service skills and a service orientation. Second, for selection, they should employ social science tools to measure applicants' attitudes and dispositions toward community-oriented policing styles, procedural justice, and interpersonal communication skills.

Psychological testing should reach beyond the traditional efforts to identify candidates with deficiencies such as proneness to violence, drug abuse, and dishonesty. Police psychologists have developed their own profiles of officers who have excessive force problems. The first profile listed is "Officers with personality disorders such as lack of empathy for others, and antisocial, narcissistic, and abusive tendencies" (Scrivner, 1994, p. iii). They also listed "impulsiveness," "low tolerance for frustration," and "dominant, heavy-handed patrol style that is particularly sensitive to challenge and provocation." Certainly, some individuals should not be police officers because of personality disorders. For example, multiple studies have shown that individuals with a narcissistic personality disorder feel superior to others, are self-centered, antagonistic, overly sensitive to criticism, and lack empathy for others (Orth et al., 2024). These traits would undermine the ability of police officers to provide compassionate services and de-escalate conflictual encounters.

On a more positive note, I recommend that government agencies seek out individuals who have strong interpersonal communication skills appropriate for the very difficult job of being a police officer. As I always say to my students, "[i]f you don't like talking to people, don't be a cop." Police interact with all types of people facing all types of problems, so officers must be able to adapt and respond appropriately. I offer several specific recommendations.

First, I think psychological testing should give more attention to emotional intelligence. This includes the capacity to read emotions and show empathy. There is a sizeable scholarly literature on emotional intelligence. Clearly, some individuals score higher on emotional intelligence than others, meaning they can perform well in social settings because they are aware of their own and other people's emotions, they understand the complexity of emotions, and are skilled at managing their own and other people's emotions to improve performance and achieve desired goals (Mayer et al., 2000). The field of measurement has evolved significantly (Petrides et al., 2016), so an emotional intelligence test would help with hiring decisions.

Second, because of problems with bias and discrimination that have defined nearly every crisis of police legitimacy in American history, the testing process should include the measurement of stereotypes and prejudice toward vulnerable groups.

Third, to change the police culture and reduce discrimination, the process of recruitment and selection should make diversity a higher priority. A sophisticated analysis of 2.9 million encounters involving Chicago Police patrol officers (Ba et al., 2021) found that Black and Hispanic officers made significantly fewer stops, arrests, and applications of force than white officers, especially for Black civilians. This analysis controlled for enforcement opportunities (i.e., beat, shift, month, and type of assignment), and the differences were attributed to fewer discretionary stops and arrests by Black and Hispanic officers for "petty crimes," including drug offenses. Black civilians appear to be less afraid of Black officers than white officers (Pickett et al., 2024). However, national data indicate that Black civilians do not attribute more procedural justice to Black officers than they do to white or Hispanic officers (Li & Sun, 2023). These nonsignificant differences may be due to the fact that Black and Hispanic officers are trapped between two cultures and identify with the "blue" police culture as much or more than their own racial/ethnic culture (Carbado & Richardson, 2018; Weitzer, 2000). New training and new performance metrics proposed here should minimize the adverse effects of social-ization into the predominately white police culture. In any event, greater diversity in the police force should help to tackle racism and restricted promotional opportun-ities (cf. Forman, 2017) that have limited the ability of minority officers to challenge the powerful police culture and express their racial identity.

Fourth, to reduce hypermasculinity in the police culture, the recruitment process should give special attention to female applicants, since they are more likely to interact with the public in the manner described in this Element. In the controlled Chicago study by Ba and colleagues (2021), female officers used force less often than male officers. Reviewing the literature, Lonsway and colleagues (2003, p. 2) point out that "women officers rely on a style of policing that uses less physical force, are better at defusing and de-escalating potentially violent confrontations with citizens, and are less likely to become involved in problems with use of excessive force."

Unfortunately, the United States has been unsuccessful at hiring more women (only 12 percent of the workforce), unlike Australia, Canada, and the UK. Historically, the police culture has not been supportive of female officers (Roman, 2020; Stepler, 2017), but work is underway to lower the barriers to female success in this male-dominated environment (Bumpers et al., 2024). My hope is that when female officers reach a critical mass, they will be able to change the hypermasculine culture.

7.2.6 Leadership

Police leaders are the key to successful reform. However, police leaders face many challenges (Haberfeld, 2006; Police Executive Research Forum, 2009). Too often they are involved in crisis management around police misconduct rather than engaged in strategic planning. For the mission described herein, police chiefs will need the skills and fortitude to introduce these changes and respond effectively to inevitable resistance. A new generation of police executives must be willing to take some risk with innovation, restore a clear mission regarding public trust and equitable police services, and clearly communicate the evidence-based methods that are needed to achieve this goal.

In summary, police chiefs and management will need to (1) revise policies and procedures to reflect this new procedural justice mission; (2) communicate the importance of this mission to all employees; (3) revise performance evaluation systems to give more attention to procedural justice during encounters with the public and strengthen the coaching skills of supervisors on this topic; (4) introduce new accountability meetings for commanders and supervisors with brainstorming sessions that focus on improving problematic PJ Index scores; (5) introduce new models of training for all employees with opportunities to practice procedural justice and receive supportive feedback; and (6) give more attention to interpersonal communication skills in the recruitment and selection of new officers.

Police chiefs should seek input from managers when making these organizational changes and fully engage them in the process. Chiefs can learn from the private sector regarding the creation of a corporate culture of "respectful" leadership (Meshanko, 2013), or "servant" leadership (Sipe & Frick, 2009) instead of "top-down" or "iron-fist" leadership. Also, agencies should look at the long history of research and theory on organizational behavior as applied to public management (Vasu et al., 1998), with the growing ethical obligation to the fair and just treatment of all employees. When teaching, I often showed a picture of a father spanking his son while saying, "This will teach you not to hit people!" On my desk, I have a poster that reads, "The beatings will continue until morale improves." In contrast, police managers should live by example and be role models of the behavior they expect from their employees. As Mahatma Gandhi once said, "Be the change you wish to see in the world."

Finally, I would be naive if I did not acknowledge the importance of external support from local government officials and community leaders. Many police chiefs in the past have failed at reforms because of numerous political and organizational obstacles they face (Skolnick & Fyle, 1993), and we should be aware of these challenges. Clearly, a strong working relationship with the external oversight agency involved in data collection is also essential.

7.3 Organizational Change Summary

In summary, internal changes will be needed at all levels of the organization to dramatically increase procedural justice during police-public encounters. The identity of the police should focus on guardianship and meeting the needs of persons seeking their help. Crime-fighting should continue, but "command and control" behaviors should be restricted to those rare situations where the person is persistently nonresponsive to less aggressive approaches or represents an immediate threat to self or others. The public as a whole should not be fearful of the police or view them with negative sentiment.

With the support of community leaders and government officials, police leaders must be willing to introduce difficult changes and respond to inevitable employee pushback and political interference. The benefits to all officers should be emphasized. Sophisticated AI analytics for BWC video data and contact survey data should be used to identify trends in procedural justice at the individual, supervisory, and unit levels. Supervisory interventions should be driven by a comprehensive problem-solving process that seeks to reward procedurally just behaviors and provide guidance in areas where performance could be improved. Work environments with punitive or weak supervision should be replaced by coaching, training, and positive reinforcement. Outside oversight is needed to collect and analyze the new data, and audit the police role in high-quality data collection. When we begin to "measure what matters" to the community and translate this data into organizational changes, we can expect that police behavior, police legitimacy, and public safety will improve.

I should note that accountability programs using contact survey data could easily be extended beyond direct police services to other components of our public safety system. This framework could be used to evaluate civilian units that respond to mental health crises (Beckett et al., 2021), as well as emergency call taker systems, like 911 (Goodier & Lum, 2023; Neusteter et al., 2019), where callers could be asked whether their call was handled in a procedurally just manner.

8 Research Agenda

Before widespread implementation of this new system, I would recommend some additional research and experimentation. Here are several research tasks to consider. The AI project in Dallas could be used as a starting point and the elements further refined.

(1) Identify several large police departments that are open to innovation and currently use BWCs, and invite them to participate as demonstration sites.

(2) Engage knowledgeable stakeholders (police, community, and policing scholars) to identify the procedural justice variables that should be measured with AI and the contact survey. Stakeholders should review and analyze BWC footage from a variety of complaint incidents to help refine the operational definition of procedural justice concepts like "disrespectful" or "resistance." They may identify multiple types of resistance and cooperation. These descriptions of behavioral patterns will help to refine and focus the AI training and possibly improve the wording on the contact survey. This research may also result in the refinement of important variables not traditionally measured in procedural justice research, such as officers' competence in answering questions, providing assistance, or showing compassion.

(3) Use BWC footage from participating police departments (and other agencies) to refine the AI algorithms via AI training on variables that emerge from this analysis.

(4) Drawing on existing procedural justice research and identified BWC variables, create a short contact survey that focuses on procedural justice (see Online Appendix for my suggestions).

(5) Create a PPA, independent of the participating police agencies, which will manage the data collection, analysis, and reporting of the survey findings. Skills in survey research, data analysis, auditing, and dashboards will be needed.

(6) Field test the contact survey methodology in these test sites. This would include developing a plan and policy for collecting the data by requiring officers to distribute business cards to community members with a QR code that gives them access to the online contact survey via their phone.

(7) Develop training for officers and supervisors around the new policy, emphasizing the importance of procedural justice in the new system of accountability and performance evaluation, and the benefits to them.

(8) Create an internal auditing unit (or use an existing unit) to ensure that all employees, from police officers to managers, are following the new policies and that supervisors are using data dashboards properly for EIS and interventions.

(9) Prepare for, and introduce, PJ meetings with commanders to begin the accountability process.

Clearly, such a new program would need to be implemented in stages, for example, policy development, training, data analysis, performance evaluations, and accountability meetings. Undoubtedly, agencies will face challenges and resistance when implementing something so new and different, but police leaders will need to be reasonable, transparent, bold, persistent, and procedurally just to overcome these challenges.

9 Summary and Conclusion

Nationwide, we are witnessing a new "crisis of legitimacy" with American policing and the problem is much deeper than the fatal shootings we see in the media. Community members are disappointed with the police for other reasons. Too often, constitutionally protected and vulnerable populations have been mistreated, especially people of color, the LGBTQ+ community, persons with mental illness, victims of crime, the homeless, and youth. In addition, our society has become more openly hostile toward other groups, such as immigrants, Jews, and Muslims, and expects the police to be tough on crime. Also, there are many internal obstacles to police reform and evidence-based policing (Lum & Koper, 2017).

In this Element, I have argued that most police reforms have failed because we continue to use the wrong metrics to evaluate police performance. Public officials and police agencies have yet to systematically measure what matters to the public, namely, how people are treated by the police. A large body of scientific evidence indicates that treating people in a procedurally just manner will improve police-community relations in many ways and should improve public safety.

Hence, I have proposed the systematic collection and analysis of new procedural justice data from BWCs and contact surveys. To change police culture and street-level behavior however, police organizations must use these data to identify problems in police-community interactions, propose solutions, implement those solutions, and evaluate their effectiveness. Thus, a POP approach should be used to translate this knowledge into evidence-based practice – new policy, training, supervision, and accountability at all levels of the organization.

This new management accountability system should incentivize respectful and empathetic communication. In other words, police performance evaluations, awards, and promotions should be driven *not* by the number of stops, searches, citations, and arrests performed by an officer, but rather by how the officer treats community members during their interactions. Punitive enforcement accountability should be replaced with positive service accountability.

These reforms, if carefully implemented, should benefit both the police and the communities they serve (Rosenbaum, 2024). The benefits to community members should include (1) more positive, less conflictual, and more satisfying encounters with the police; (2) greater trust and confidence in the police and support for their decision-making; (3) less cynicism about the law and greater willingness to obey the law; (4) greater willingness to work with the police to create effective crime prevention partnerships; (5) less desire to file complaints and lawsuits; (6) increased public safety as a result of these changes; and (7) fewer taxpayer dollars spent on lawsuits against police officers.

For police officers, I envision many benefits that should lower police resistance to this type of innovation and improve their effectiveness in fighting crime. By learning stronger procedural justice, de-escalation, and communication skills, police officers should experience (1) more successful criminal investigations as a result of more cooperative witnesses, victims, bystanders, callers, and suspects, thus producing greater justice and deterrence; (2) more cooperative community members and fewer use of force incidents; (3) fewer misconduct complaints and investigations, thus reducing officers' fear of punishment; (4) fewer officer safety and mental health problems; (5) greater job satisfaction and less cynicism toward their agency and the community; (6) less "de-policing," resulting in more crime prevention and increased public safety; and (7) greater agency legitimacy, resulting in fewer protests, negative social media, lawsuits, and defunding campaigns.

9.1 Big Science

In the future, I envision a national system of procedural justice measurement where thousands of agencies are participating. This should become a cost-effective system where cities share the costs and benefits of this program. The costs include data collection and auditing functions, while the benefits would include implementation integrity, data analysis needed for accountability dashboards, and eventually, increased public trust and legitimacy. Another big benefit for science at large is the knowledge generated from conducting intercity comparisons and using city and police demographics as the unit of analysis. As I pointed out earlier, procedural justice varies by agency size. The question is why and what can we learn from these differences?

In the meantime, we need to see a proof-of-concept demonstration and rigorous evaluation in multiple cities. This should involve a genuine partnership among police leaders, policing scholars, and community leaders, with funding from the government and foundations. The result should be a standardized, validated, cost-effective set of metrics and analytics, along with specific, evidence-based organizational changes needed to translate this knowledge into efficient, effective, and equitable policing.

Weisburd and his colleagues (2024) have called for the introduction of "Big Science" with large-scale investments to address the SQF problem. I agree with this recommendation, but would expand the national research agenda to include police-community interactions in general. Big Science should be used to investigate new ways of measuring the effects of police-community interactions and translating this knowledge into practice. After the systems have been developed and field tested for implementation integrity, a large-scale demonstration and evaluation should be funded across multiple cities, including randomized trials to test different methods of implementation. This foundational work is essential for advancing our understanding of police-community encounters and introducing evidence-based policing that will improve procedural justice, police legitimacy, and public safety. Then, we should be ready for a national rollout to all law enforcement agencies in the United States. Welcome to Big Science in the field of policing!

References

60 Minutes. (2024). CBS News, December 29, *60 Minutes*, S57 Ep16. www.cbsnews.com/video/nvidia-ceo-jensen-huang-60-minutes-video-2024-12-29/.

Abrams, K. (1999). From autonomy to agency: Feminist perspectives on self-direction. *William & Mary Law Review*, 40(3), 805–846. https://scholarship.law.wm.edu/wmlr/vol40/iss3/6.

Ahrens, C. E. (2006). Being silenced: The impact of negative social reactions on the disclosure of rape. *American Journal of Psychology*, 38, 263–274. https://doi.org/10.1007/s10464-006-9069-9.

Alabama Appleseed Center for Law & Justice. (2023). *Taken for a ride: How excessive ticketing propels Alabama drivers into a cycle of debt, incarceration, and poverty.* alabamaappleseed.org/wp-content/uploads/2023/07/Alabama-Appleseed-Taken-for-a-RideReport-2023-WEB.pdf.

Albert, S., & de Ruiter, J. P. (2018). Repair: The interface between interaction and cognition. *Topics in Cognitive Science*, 10, 279–313. Published by Wiley Periodicals. https://onlinelibrary.wiley.com/doi/pdf/10.1111/tops.12339.

Alexander, M. (2011). *The new Jim Crow: Mass incarceration in the age of colorblindness.* The New Press.

Alexander, K. L., Rich, S., & Thacker, H. (2022). The hidden billion-dollar cost of repeated police misconduct. *Washington Post*, March 9. www.washingtonpost.com/investigations/interactive/2022/police-misconduct-repeated-settlements/#.

Allport, G. (1954). *The nature of prejudice.* Reading: Addison-Wesley Pub. Co. ISBN 0-201-00179-9.

Alpert, G. P., & Moore, M. H. (1993). Measuring police performance in the new paradigm of policing. In G. P. Alpert & A. R. Piquero (Eds.), *Community policing: Contemporary readings.* (pp. 215–232). Waveland Press.

Antrobus, E., Thompson, I., & Ariel, B. (2019). Procedural justice training for police recruits: Results of a randomized controlled trial. *Journal of Experimental Criminology*, 15(1), 29–53. https://doi.org/10.1007/s11292-018-9331-9.

Asher, J., & Horwitz, B. (2021). How do the police actually spend their time? *New York Times*, November 8. www.nytimes.com/2020/06/19/upshot/unrest-police-time-violent-crime.html.

Ayers, J. W., Poliak, A., Dredze, M. et al. (2023). Comparing physician and artificial intelligence chatbot responses to patient questions posted to a public social media forum. *JAMA Intern Med*, June 1; 183(6), 589–596. https:// pubmed.ncbi.nlm.nih.gov/37115527/.

Ba, B., Kaplan, J., Knox, D., Komisarchik, M., Lanzalotto, G. et al. (2023). Political diversity in US police agencies. Google Scholar.

Ba, B. A., Knox, D., Mummolo, J., & Rivera, R. (2021). The role of officer race and gender in police-civilian interactions in Chicago, *Science*, 371(6530), 696–702. https://doi.org/10.1126/science.abd8694.

Baddeley, A., Eysenck, M. W., & Anderson, A. C. (2009). *Memory*. Psychology Press.

Balko, R. (2014). *Rise of the Warrior Cop: The militarization of American's police forces*. Public Affairs.

Bandura, A. (1997). *Self-Efficacy: The exercise of control*. Freeman.

Bandura, A. (2006). Toward a psychology of human agency. *Perspectives on Psychological Science*, 1(2), 164–180.

Barker, K., Keller, M. H., & Eder, S. (2021). How cities lost control of police discipline. *New York Times*, March 10. www.nytimes.com/2020/12/22/us/ police-misconduct-discipline.html.

Barrouillet, P., & Camos, V. (2012). As time goes by: Temporal constraints in working memory. *Current Directions in Psychological Science*, 21(6), 413–419. https://doi.org/10.1177/0963721412459513.

Baum, A., Fisher, J. D., & Singer, J. E. (1985). *Social psychology*. Random House.

Baumgartner, F. R., Epp, D. A., & Shoub, K. (2018). *Suspect citizens: What 20 million traffic stops tell us about policing and race*. Cambridge University Press.

Beckett, K., Stuart, F., & Bell, M. (2021). *From crisis to care. Inquest*, September 2. https://inquest.org/from-crisis-to-care/.

Bedmutha, M. S., Bascom, E., Sladek, K. R. et al. (2024). Artificial intelligence-generated feedback on social signals in patient-provider com- munication: Technical performance, feedback usability, and impact. *JAMIA Open*. October 18; 7(4), ooae106. https://pubmed.ncbi.nlm.nih.gov/ 39430803/.

Bello, M. (2014). "It can be fearful": Police feeling under siege. *USA Today*, December 24, A15 pp, www.usatoday.com/story/news/nation/2014/12/22/ police-react-shootings/20773395/.

BenitezSantiago, A. B., & Miltenberger, R. G. (2015). Using video feedback to improve martial arts performance. *Behavioral Interventions*, 31(1), 12–27. https://doi.org/10.1002/bin.1424.

Bickman, L., Lyons, A., & Wolpert, M. (2016). Achieving precision mental health through effective assessment, monitoring, and feedback processes.

Administration and Policy in Mental Health and Mental Health Services Research, 43, 271–276. https://doi.org/10.1007/s1048 8-016-0718-5.

Bittner, E. (1970). *The functions of the police in modern society.* National Institute of Mental Health.

Blumstein, A. (1999). Measuring what matters in policing. In R. Langworthy (Ed.), *Measuring what matters: Proceedings from the policing research institute meetings.* (pp. 5–10). National Institute of Justice and Office of Community Oriented Policing Services.

Bolger, M. A., Lytle, D. J., & Bolger, P. C. (2021). What matters in citizen satisfaction with police: A meta-analysis. *Journal of Criminal Justice Volume*, 72, January–February. https://doi.org/10.1016/j.jcrimjus.2020.101760.

Bolger, P. C., & Walters, G. D. (2019). The relationship between police procedural justice, police legitimacy, and people's willingness to cooperate with law enforcement: A meta-analysis. *Journal of Criminal Justice*, 60, 93–99. https://doi.org/10.1016/j.jcrimjus.2019.01.001.CrossRefGoogle Scholar

Bolton, R. (1985). *People Skills*. Prentice Hall.

Bradford, B. (2014). Policing and social identity: Procedural justice, inclusion and cooperation between police and public. *Policing and Society*, 24(1), 22–43. https://doi.org/10.1080/10439463.2012.724068.

Bradford, B., Murphy, K., & Jackson, J. (2014). Officers as mirrors: Policing, procedural Justice and the (re) production of social identity. *British Journal of Criminology*, 54(4), 527–550. https://doi.org/10.1093/bjc/azu021.

Braga. A. A., & Weisburd, D. (2019). Problem-Oriented policing: The disconnect between principles and practice. In D. Weisburd & A. A. Braga (Eds.), *Police innovation: Contrasting perspectives.* (2nd Ed., pp. 182–202). Cambridge University Press.

Braga, A. A., Turchan, B., Papachristos, A. V., & Hureau, D. M. (2019). Hot spots policing of small geographic areas effects on crime. September 8. *Campbell Systematic Reviews*.

Bratton, W. (1999). Great expectations: How higher expectations for police departments can lead to a decrease in crime. In R. H. Langworthy (Ed.), *Measuring what matters: Proceedings from the policing research institute meetings.* (pp. 11–26). National Institute of Justice.

Brehm, S. S., & Brehm, J. W. (2013). *Psychological reactance: A theory of freedom and control.* Academic Press.

Bridges, V. (2024). North Carolina police turn to training to stop taser misuse. *The Charlotte Observer*, December 5. www.govtech.com/em/safety/north carolina police-turn-to-training-to-stop-taser-misuse.

Brown, B., & Benedict, W. R. (2002). Perceptions of the police: Past findings, methodological issues, conceptual issues and policy implications. *Policing:*

An International Journal of Police Strategies and Management, 25(3), 543–580. https://doi.org/10.1108/13639510210437032.

Buehler, E. D. (2021). *Justice Expenditures and Employment in the United States, 2017*. Bureau of Justice Statistics, Office of Justice Programs, U.S. Department of Justice. July 2021, NCJ 256093.

Bumpers, V., Manigault, D., & Winstead, D. (Eds.) (2024). Women in policing. *Police Chief Magazine*, March Issue. International Association of Chiefs of Police. www.policechiefmagazine.org/magazine-issues/march-2024-women-in-policing/.

Bushway, S. (1996). *The impact of a criminal history record on access to legitimate employment*. Unpublished doctoral dissertation. H. John Heinz School of Public Policy and Management, Carnegie Mellon University.

Carbado, D. W., & Richardson, L. S. (2018). The Black police: Policing our own. Book review of Forman, J. Jr. (2017). *Locking Up Our Own: Crime and Punishment in Black America. Harvard Law Review*, 131(7), 1979–2025. https://harvardlawreview.org/print/vol-131/the-black-police-policing-our-own/.

Carmichael, J., David, J., Helou, A., & Pereira, C. (2021). Determinants of citizens' perceptions of police behavior during traffic and pedestrian stops. *Criminal Justice Review*, 46(1), 99–118.

Cavanagh, N., Cockett, G., Heinrich, C. et al. (2020). Compassion fatigue in healthcare providers: A systematic review and meta-analysis. *Nursing Ethics*, 27(3), 639–665. https://doi.org/10.1177/0969733019889400.

Chen, Y., Chen, X., & Portnoy, R. (2009). To whom do positive norm and negative norm of reciprocity apply? Effects of inequitable offer, relationship, and relational-self orientation. *Journal of Experimental Social Psychology*, 45(1), 24–34.

Clampitt, P. G. (1991). *Communicating for managerial effectiveness*. Sage.

Confessore, N. (2024). America is under attack: Inside the anti-D.E.I. crusade. *New York Times*, January 20. www.nytimes.com/interactive/2024/01/20/us/dei-woke-claremont-institute.html.

Cordner, G. W. (1997). Community policing: Elements and effects. In G. P. Alpert & A. R. Piquero (Eds.), *Community policing: Contemporary readings*. (pp. 45–62). Waveland Press.

Cordner, G. W. (2017). Police culture: Individual and organizational differences in police officer perspectives. *Policing: An International Journal*, 40(1), 11–25. https://doi.org/10.1108/PIJPSM-07-2016-0116.

Covey, T. J., Shucard, J. L., Violanti, J. M., et al. (2023). The effects of exposure to traumatic stressors on inhibitory control in police officers: A dense electrode array study using a Go/NoGo continuous performance task.

International Journal of Psychophysiology, 87(3), 363–375. https://doi.org/10.1016/j.ijpsycho.2013.03.009.

Craddock, T. B., & Telesco, G. (2022). Police stress and deleterious outcomes: Efforts towards improving police mental health. *Journal of Police and Criminal Psychology*, 37(1), 173–182. https://doi.org/10.1007/s11896-021-09488-1.

Crank, J. P., & Langworthy, R. (1992). An institutional perspective of policing. *The Journal of Criminal Law and Criminology*, 83, 338–363.

Danish, S. J., & Ferguson, N. (1973). Training police to intervene in human conflict. In J. R. Snibbe & H. M. Snibbe (Eds.), *The urban policeman in transition: A psychological and sociological review.* (pp. 486–506). Charles C Thomas.

Davies, E. (2022). In this small Va. town, citizens review police like Uber drivers. *The Washington Post*. June 2. www.washingtonpost.com/dc-md-va/2022/06/02/warrenton-virginia-police-reviews/.

Deck, S. L., Porter, L. E., Powell, M., & Alpert, G. (2024). Police recruits' perceptions of the utility of body-worn cameras as a training tool. *Criminal Justice and Behavior*, 1–16. https://doi.org/10.1177/00938548241302478.

Decker, S. H. (1981). Citizen attitudes toward the police: A review of past findings and suggestions for future policy. *Journal of Police Science and Administration*, 9, 80–87. Google Scholar.

Department of Justice (2024). *Investigation of the Memphis Police Department and the City of Memphis*. Washington DC: United States Department of Justice, Civil Rights Division and United States Attorney's Office, Western District of Tennessee, Civil Division. December 4. www.justice.gov/crt/media/1379096/dl?inlinet.

DeVylder, J. E., Oh, H. Y., Nam, B. 1. et al. (2017). Prevalence, demographic variation, and psychological correlates of exposure to police victimization in four U.S. cities. *Epidemiological and Psychiatric Sciences*, 26, 466–477. https://doi.org/10.1017/S245796016000810.

Dholakia, N. (2022). Most 911 calls have nothing to do with crime. Why are we still sending police? Vera Institute of Justice. April 22. www.vera.org/news/most-911-calls-have-nothing-to-do-with-crime-why-are-we-still-sending-police.

Dolly, C., Hansen, E., Gallardo, R. et al. (2024). *Multi-modal analysis of body-worn camera recordings: Evaluating novel methods for measuring police implementation of procedural justice.* Final report to the National Institute of Justice, Award # 2020-R2-CX-0010.

Donner, C. M., Maskaly, J., Fridell, L., & Jennings, W. G. (2015). Policing and procedural justice. *Policing*, 38, 153–172. Google Scholar.

D'Souza, A., Weitzer, R., & Brunson, R. K. (2019). Federal investigations of police misconduct: A multi-city comparison. *Crime, Law and Social Change*, 71, 461–482.

Du Bois, W. E. B. (1903). The souls of Black folk. *The Project Gutenberg eBook*. www.gutenberg.org/files/408/408-h/408-h.htm#chap15.

Dulaney, W. M. (2015). The troubled origins of American policing. *The Crime Report*. May 19. https://thecrimereport.org/2015/05/19/2015-05-the-troubled-origins-of-american-policing/.

Dunklin, R., Foley, R. J., Martin, J. et al. (2024). Why did more than 1,000 people die after police subdued them with force that isn't meant to kill? *Associated Press*. March 28. https://apnews.com/article/associated-press-investigation-deaths-police-encounters-02881a2bd3fbeb1fc31af9208bb0e310.

Dunworth, T., Cordner, G., Greene, J. et al. (2000). *Police department information systems technology enhancement project ISTEP*. U.S. Department of Justice, Office of Community Oriented Policing Services.

Eck, J. E., & Rosenbaum, D. P. (1994). The new police order: Effectiveness, equity, and efficiency in community policing. In D. P. Rosenbaum (Ed.), *The challenge of community policing: Testing the promises*. (pp. 3–23). Sage.

Eck, J. E., & Spelman, W. (1987). *Problem solving: Problem-oriented policing in Newport News*. Police Executive Research Forum.

Edsall, T. B. (2024). Two opposing developments that changed American politics. Guest Essay, Opinion Section. *New York Times*, August 7. www.nytimes.com/2024/08/07/opinion/trump-harris-black-lives-matter.html?searchResultPosition=3.

Elfers, T., Martin, J., & Sokol, B. (2008). Perspective taking: A review of research and theory extending Selman's developmental model of perspective taking. In A. M. Columbus (Ed.), *Advances in psychology research*. (pp. 229–262). Nova Science.

Elliott, I., Thomas, S., & Ogloff, J. (2012). Procedural justice in contacts with the police: The perspective of victims of crime. *Police Practice and Research*, 13, 437–449. https://doi.org/10.1080/15614263.2011.607659.

Engel, R. (2001). Supervisory styles of patrol sergeants and lieutenants. *Journal of Criminal Justice*, 29, 341–355.

Engel, R. S., & Calnon, J. M. (2004). Examining the influence of drivers' characteristics during traffic stops with police: Results from a national survey. *Justice Quarterly*, 21(1), 49–90. https://doi.org/10.1080/07418820400095741.

Engel, R. S., & Eck, J. E. (2015). Effectiveness vs. equity in policing: Is a tradeoff inevitable? *Ideas in American Policing* series, No. 18, National Policing Institute. www.policinginstitute.org/wp-content/uploads/2015/09/PF_IIAP_EngelandEck_Jan2015.pdf.

Engel, R. S., & Swartz, K. (2014). Race, crime, and policing. In S. M. Bucerius & M. Tonry (Eds.), *Oxford handbook of ethnicity, crime, and immigration.* (pp. 135–165). Oxford Press.

Epp, C. R., Maynard-Moody, S., & Haider-Markel, D. (2014). *Pulled over: How police stops define race and citizenship.* University of Chicago Press.

Evans, F. (2021). The 1967 riots: When outrage over racial Injustice boiled over. *History* (H). www.history.com/news/1967-summer-riots-detroit-newark-kerner-commission.

Farooq, U. (2024). Police departments are turning to AI to sift through millions of hours of unreviewed body-cam footage. *PROPUBLICA.* February 2. www.propublica.org/article/police-body-cameras-video-ai-law-enforcement.

Fielding, J. (2022). Outlawing police quotas. *Brennan Center for Justice.* July 13. www.brennancenter.org/our-work/analysis-opinion/outlawing-police-quotas.

Forman, J. Jr. (2017). *Locking up our own: Crime and punishment in Black America.* Farrar, Straus and Giroux.

Foster, J. T., Zimmerman, L., Terrill, W., & Somers, L. J. (2024). Finding the path of least resistance: An examination of officer communication tactics and their impact on suspect compliance. *Criminology & Public Policy,* 23, 639–662.

Fridell, L. (2004). By the Numbers: A guide for analyzing race data from vehicle stops. *The Police Executive Research Forum.*

Fridell, L. (2008). Racially biased policing: The law enforcement response to the implicit Black-crime association. In M. J. Lynch, E. B. Patterson, & K. K. Childs (Eds.), *Racial divide: Racial and ethnic bias in the criminal justice system.* (pp. 39–59). Criminal Justice Press.

Fridell, L. A. (2017). *Producing bias-free policing: A science-based approach.* Springer.

Fridell, L. A., & Wycoff, M. A. (2004, Eds.) *Community policing: The past, present and future.* Police Executive Research Forum. www.policeforum.org/assets/docs/Free_Online_Documents/Community_Policing/community%20policing%20-%20the%20past%20present%20and%20future%202004.pdf.

Gascon, L. D., & Roussell, A. (2019). *The limits of community policing: Civilian power and police accountability in Black and Brown Los Angeles.* New York University Press.

Gau, J. M. (2014). Organizational change and police legitimacy. *Encyclopedia of Criminology and Criminal Justice.* Springer.

Gau, J. M. (2015). Procedural justice, police legitimacy, and legal cynicism: A test for mediation effects. *Police Practice and Research,* 16, 402–415. https://doi.org/10.1080/15614263.2014.927766.

Gau, J. M., & Brunson, R. K. (2010). Procedural justice and order maintenance policing: A study of inner-city young men's perceptions of police legitimacy. *Justice Quarterly*, 27(2), 255–279. https://doi.org/10.1080/07418820 902763889.

Geller, A. (2021). Youth-police contact: Burdens and inequities in an adverse childhood experience, 2014–2017. *American Journal of Public Health*, 111(7), 1300–1308. http://doi.org/10.2105/AJPH.2021.306259.

Geller, A., & Mark, N. (2022). Student absenteeism and the role of police encounters. *Criminology and Public Policy*, 21, 893–914. https://doi.org/10.1111/1745-9133.12600.

Gladwell, M. (2005). *Blink: The power of thinking without thinking*. Back Bay Books, Little, Brown.

Gladwell, M. (2019). *Talking to strangers: What we should know about the people we don't know*. Back Bay Books, Little, Brown.

Goldstein, H. (1979). Improving policing: A problem oriented approach. *Crime and Delinquency*, 24, 236–258.

Goldstein, H. (1990). *Problem-oriented policing*. McGraw-Hill.

Goodier, M., & Lum, C. (2023). First point of contact: Can procedural justice be applied by emergency calltakers? *Policing: A Journal of Policy and Practice*, 17, paac102, https://doi.org/10.1093/police/paac102.

Gouldner, A. (1960). The norm of reciprocity: A preliminary statement. *American Sociological Review*. 25(2), 161–178.

Graham, M. A. (2024). Compounding anti-Black racial disparities in police stops. *Center for Policing Equity*. October. https://policingequity.org/traffic-safety.

Graham, M. A., Neath, S., Buchanan, K. S., et al. (2024). Racial disparities in use of force at traffic stops. *Center for Policing Equity*. https://policingequity.org/traffic-safety.

Gramlich, J. (2024). What the data says about crime in the U.S. *Pew Research Center*. April 24. www.pewresearch.org/short-reads/2024/04/24/what-the-data-says-about-crime-in-the-us/.

Grant, H. B., & Terry, K. J. (2005). *Law enforcement in the 21st century*. Allyn and Bacon.

Green, J. R., & Mastrofski, S. D. (1988, Eds.). *Community policing: Rhetoric or reality?* Praeger.

Grossman, D., & Christensen, L. W. (2008). *On Combat: The psychology and physiology of deadly conflict in war and in peace*. Human Factors Research Group.

Haar, R. N. (2000). The impact of community policing training and program Implementation on police personnel. Final report for the National Institute of

Justice, grant number 96-IJ-CX-0060. *National Institute of Justice*. NCJ 190680.

Haberfeld, M. R. (2006). *Police leadership*. Pearson Education.

Harrell, E., & Davis, E. (2020). Contacts between police and the public, 2018 – Statistical Tables. *Bureau of Justice Statistics*, U.S. Department of Justice. NCJ 255730. https://bjs.ojp.gov/library/publications/contacts-between-police-and-public-2018-statistical-tables.

Hernandez, A. (2024). "Tough-on-crime" policies are back in some places that had reimagined criminal justice. *Daily Montanan*. April 15. https://dailymon tanan.com/2024/04/15/tough-on-crime-policies-are-back-in-some-places-that-had-reimagined-criminal-justice/.

Hinkle, J. C., Weisburd, D., Telep, C. W., & Petersen, K. (2020). Problem-oriented policing for reducing crime and disorder: An updated systematic review and meta-analysis. *Campbell Systematic Review*, June 15.

Hohl, K., Reid, A.-K., Molisso, S., & Pullerits, M. (2024). *Rape and sexual assault survivors' experience of the police in England and Wales. Survey Report I: January – June 2023*. City, University of London.

Hohl, K., & Stanko, E. A. (2024). *Policing rape: The way forward*. Taylor & Francis. https://doi.org/10.4324/9780429444869.

Hough, M., Jackson, J., & Bradford, B. (2013). Legitimacy, trust, and compliance: An empirical test of procedural justice theory using the European social survey. In J. Tankebe & A. Liebling (Eds.), *Legitimacy and criminal justice: An international exploration.* (pp. 326–352). Oxford University Press. Google Scholar.

Johnson, M. S. (2003). *Street justice: A history of police violence in New York City*. Beacon Press.

Jonathan-Zamir, T., Perry, G., Kaplan-Damary, N., & Weisburd, D. (2024). Police compliance with the social contract as an antecedent of police legitimacy, of satisfaction with the police, and of willingness to obey: Findings from a two-stage vignette experiment. *Journal of Experimental Criminology*. https://doi.org/10.1007/s11292-024-09622-z.

Kappeler, V. E., Sluder, R. D., & Alpert, G. P. (1998). *Forces of deviance: Understanding the dark side of policing*. Waveland Press.

Katz, R., & Kahn, R. (1966). *The social psychology of organizations*. Wiley and Sons.

Kanov, J. M., Maitlis, S., Worline, M. C., et al. (2004). Compassion in organizational life, *American Behavioral Scientist*, 47(6), 808–827. DOI: 10.1177/0002764203260211. Sage.

Kegler, S. R., Simon, T. R., & Sumner, S. A. (2023). Notes from the field: Firearm homicide rates, by race and ethnicity – United States, 2019–2022.

(*MMWR*) *Morbidity and Mortality Weekly Report*, 72(42), 1149–1150. http://dx.doi.org/10.15585/mmwr.mm7242a4.

Kelly, J., & Nichols, M. (2020). We found 85,000 cops who've been investigated for misconduct. *USA TODAY*, April 24. www.usatoday.com/in-depth/news/investigations/2019/04/24/usa-today-revealing-misconduct-records-police-cops/3223984002/.

Kirk, D., & Papachristos, A. (2011). Cultural mechanisms and the persistence of neighborhood violence. *American Journal of Sociology*, 116, 1190–1233.

Kirkpatrick, D. D., Eder, S., Barker, K., & Tate, J. (2021). Pulled over: Why many police traffic stops turn deadly. *New York Times*, October 31. www.nytimes.com/2021/10/31/us/police-traffic-stops-killings.html.

Klein, M. W. (1986). Labeling theory and delinquency policy: An empirical test. *Criminal Justice and Behavior*, 13, 47–79.

Klinger, D. (1997). Negotiating order in patrol work: An ecological theory of police response to deviance. *Criminology*, 35(2), 277–306.

Klose, S. (2024). Re-defining evidence-based policing. *Policing: A Journal of Policy and Practice*, 18, paad095, https://doi.org/10.1093/police/paad095.

Kochel, T. R., Wilson, D. B., & Mastrofski, S. D. (2011). Effect Of suspect race on officers' arrest decisions. *Criminology*, 49(2), 473–512. https://doi.org/10.1111/j.1745-9125.2011.00230.x.

Lang, M., Xygalatas, D., Kavanagh, C. M. et al. (2021). Outgroup threat and the emergence of cohesive groups: A cross-cultural examination. *Group Processes & Intergroup Relations*, 25(7), 1–21. https://doi.org/10.1177/13684302211016961. www.researchgate.net/publication/353379093_Outgroup_threat_and_the_emergence_of_cohesive_groups_A_cross-cultural_examination.

Langton, L., & Durose, M. R. (2013). *Police behavior during traffic and street stops, 2011*. Bureau of Justice Statistics, U.S. Department of Justice. NCJ No. 242938. https://bjs.ojp.gov/library/publications/police-behavior-during-traffic-and-street-stops-2011.

Langworthy, R. H. (1999, Ed.). *Measuring what matters: Proceedings from the Policing Research Institute Meetings*. National Institute of Justice and the Office of Community Oriented Policing Services, U.S. Department of Justice. NCJ 170610-1.

La Vigne, N. (2022). Can early intervention prevent police misconduct? *The Crime Report*. January 25. Center on Media, Crime, & Justice, John Jay College of Criminal Justice. https://thecrimereport.org/2022/01/25/can-early-intervention-prevent-at-risk-officers-from-committing-misconduct/.

La Vigne, N. (2024). Public criminology: Charting the course from evidence to action. *Translational Criminology*, Fall Issue, George Mason University. https://cebcp.org/wp-content/uploads/2024/10/TC24-Fall2024.pdf.

Lawrence, S., & Cole, C. (2019). *Building capacity: How police departments can drive positive changes without Federal Intervention*. Crime and Justice Institute, Community Resources for Justice. www.cjinstitute.org/publication/building-capacity-how-police-departments-can-drive-positive-change-without-federal-intervention/.

Leathers, G. J. (1992). *Successful nonverbal communication: Principles and applications*, 2nd ed. Macmillan.

Lerman, A. E., & Weaver, V. M. (2014). *Arresting citizenship: The democratic consequences of American Crime Control*. University of Chicago Press.

Li, L., & Sun, I. Y. (2023). Procedural justice and police legitimacy: Untangling the effects of racial and ethnic combinations between the police and civilians. *Criminal Justice Review*, 0(0). https://doi.org/10.1177/07340168231218944.

Lind, E. A., & Tyler, T. R. (1988). *Social psychology of procedural justice*. Plenum Press.

Lofstrom, M., Hayes, J., Martin, B., & Premkumar, D. (2022). *Racial disparities in traffic stops*. October, Public Policy Institute of California. www.ppic.org/?show-pdf=true&docraptor=true&url=https%3A%2F%2Fwww.ppic.org%2Fpublication%2Fracial-disparities-in-traffic-stops%2F.

Lonsway, K., Moore, M., Harrington, P., Smeal, E., & Spillar, K. (2003). *Hiring and retaining more women: The Advantages to Law Enforcement*. National Center for Women & Policing.

Lorenz, K. (2017). *Reporting sexual assault to police: Victim experiences and the potential for procedural justice*. PhD Dissertation, University of Illinois at Chicago.

Love-Koh, J., Peel, A., Rejon-Parrilla, J. C. et al. (2018). The future of precision medicine: Potential impacts for health technology assessment. *Pharmaco-Economics*, 36(12), 1439–1451. https://doi.org/10.1007/s40273-018-0686-6.

Lum, C. (2021). Perspectives on policing. *Annual Review of Criminology*, 4, 19–25.

Lum, C., & Koper, C. S. (2017). *Evidence-based policing: Translating research into practice*. Oxford University Press.

Lum, C., Koper, C. S., Wilson, D. B. et al. (2020). Body-worn cameras' effects on police officers and citizen behavior: A systematic review. *Campbell Systematic Reviews*, 16(3), e1112. https://doi.org/10.1002/cl2.1112.

Lum, C., & Nagin, D. S. (2017). Reinventing American policing. In M. Tonry & D. S. Nagin (Eds.), *Crime and justice*, 46(1), 339–393. University of Chicago

Press. https://cebcp.org/wp-content/uploads/2020/06/2017-Lum-and-Nagin-Reinventing-American-Policing.pdf.

Lum, C., Stoltz, M., Koper, C. S., & Scherer, J. A. (2019). The research on body-worn cameras: What we know, what we need to know. *Criminology and Public Policy*, 18(1), 93–118. http://doi.org/10.1111/1745-9133.12412.

Lynch, S. N., & Goudsward, A. (2024). Biden's Justice Dept has yet to reach accords in police misconduct cases. October 29. *Reuters*. www.reuters.com/legal/bidens-justice-dept-has-yet-reach-accords-police-misconduct-cases-2024-10-29/.

Lyons, W. (1999). *The politics of community policing: Rearranging the power to punish*. University of Michigan Press. https://doi.org/10.3998/mpub.15188.

MacQueen, S., & Bradford, B. (2015). Enhancing public trust and police legitimacy during road traffic encounters: Results from a randomised controlled trial in Scotland. *Journal of Experimental Criminology*, 11(3), 419–443.

MacQueen, S., & Bradford, B. (2017). Where did it all go wrong? Implementation failure – and more – in a field experiment of procedural justice policing. *Journal of Experimental Criminology*, 13(3), 321–345.

Maguire, E. R. (1997). Structural change in large municipal police organizations during the community policing era. *Justice Quarterly*, 14, 547–576.

Maguire, E. R. (2004a). Measuring the performance of law enforcement agencies: Part two. *Commission on Accreditation for Law Enforcement Agencies*, 84. www.calea.org/newweb/newsletter/No84/maguirepart2.htm.

Maguire, E. R. (2004b). Police departments as learning laboratories. *Ideas in American policing* lecture series. No. 6. National Policing Institute. www.policinginstitute.org/publication/police-departments-as-learning-laboratories.

Maguire, E. R., & Lowrey, B. V. (2017). Evaluating the relative impact of positive and negative encounters with police: A randomized experiment. *Journal of Experimental Criminology*, 13, 367–391. https://doi.org/10.1007/s11292-016-9276-9.

Maguire, E. R., Lowrey-Kinberg, B., & Johnson, D. (2023). The role of anger in mediating the effects of procedural justice and injustice. *Group Processes & Intergroup Relations*, 26(4), 796–815. https://doi.org/10.1177/13684302221115640.

Masterson, M. F., & Stevens, D. J. (2002). The value of measuring community policing performance in Madison, Wisconsin. In D. J. Stevens (Ed.), *Policing and community partnerships*. (pp. 202–217). Prentice Hall.

Mastrofski, S. D. (1999). Policing for people. Ideas in American policing, March Issue. *National Policing Institute*. www.policinginstitute.org/wp-content/uploads/2015/06/Mastrofski-1999-Policing-For-People.pdf.

Mastrofski, S. D. (2019). Community policing: A skeptical view. In D. Weisburd & A. A. Braga (Eds.), *Police innovation: Contrasting perspectives*. (2nd Ed., pp. 45–68). Cambridge University Press.

Mastrofski, S. D., Reisig, M. D., & McCluskey, J. D. (2002). Police disrespect toward the public: An encounter-based analysis. *Criminology*, 40(3), 519–552.

Mayer, J. D., Salovey, P., & Caruso, D. R. (2000). Models of emotional intelligence. In R. J. Sternberg (Ed.), *Handbook of intelligence*. (pp. 396–420). Cambridge University Press.

Mazerolle, L., Antrobus, E., Bennett, S., & Tyler, T. (2013b). Shaping citizen perceptions of police legitimacy: A randomized field trial of procedural justice. *Criminology*, 51, 33–63. https://doi.org/10.1111/J.1745-9125.2012.00289.X.

Mazerolle, L., Bennett, S., Antrobus, E., & Eggins, E. (2012). Procedural justice, routine encounters and citizen perceptions of police: Main findings from the Queensland Community Engagement Trial (QCET). *Journal of Experimental Criminology*, 8(4), 343–367.

Mazerolle, L., Bennett, S., Davis, J., Sargeant, E., & Manning, M. (2013a). Procedural justice and police legitimacy: A systematic review of the research evidence. *Journal of Experimental Criminology*, 9, 245–274. https://doi.org/10.1007/S11292-013-9175-2.

Mazerolle, L., Sargeant, E., Cherney, A. et al. (2014). *Procedural justice and legitimacy in policing*. Springer. Google Scholar.

McAward, A. (2022). Law enforcement officer suicides: Risk factors and limitations on data analysis. *American College of Emergency Physicians*, Tactical and Law Enforcement Medicine Section. January 10. www.acep.org/talem/newsroom/january-2022/law-enforcement-officer-suicides–risk-factors-and-limitations-on-data-analysis/.

McCann, S. (2023). Low-level traffic stops are ineffective – and sometimes deadly. Why are they still happening? *News and Stories*, Vera Institute of Justice, March 29. www.vera.org/news/low-level-traffic-stops-are-ineffective-and-sometimes-deadly-why-are-they-still-happening#:~:text=According%20to%20Baumgartner's%20research%2C%20it,of%20less%20than%20one%20percent.

McCarthy, G. F., & Rosenbaum, D. P. (2015). From CompStat to RespectStat: Accountability for respectful policing. *The Police Chief*, August, 76–77. www.policechiefmagazine.org/from-compstat-to-respectstat-accountability-for-respectful-policing/.

McGarty, C., Yzerbyt, V. Y., & Spears, R. (2002). *Stereotypes as explanations: The formation of meaningful beliefs about social groups*. Cambridge University Press. ISBN 978-0-521-80047-1.

Meares, T. L. (2014). The law and social science of stop and frisk. *Annual Review of Law and Social Science*, 10(1), 335–352. https://doi.org/10.1146/annurev-lawsocsci-102612-134043.

Meichenbaum, D. (1984). Teaching thinking: A cognitive-behavioral perspective. In R. Glaser, S. Chipman, & J. Segal (Eds.), *Thinking and learning skills: Vol. 2. research and open questions.* (pp. 407–426). Erlbaum.

Meshanko, P. (2013). *The respect effect: Using the science of neuroleadership to inspire a more loyal and productive workplace*. McGaw Hill Education.

Mirzer, M. L. (1996). Policing supervision in the 21st century. *FBI Law Enforcement Bulletin*, 65(6), 6–10.

Monnay, T. (2022). States approved nearly 300 bills affecting policing in wake of George Floyd's murder. The Howard Center for Investigative Journalism, Philip Merrill College of Journalism. October 28. https://cnsmaryland.org/2022/10/28/states-approved-nearly-300-bills-affecting-policing-in-wake-of-george-floyds-murder/.

Moore, M. H., & Poethig, M. (1999). The police as an agency of municipal government: Implications for measuring police effectiveness. In R. H. Langworthy (Ed.), *Measuring what matters: Proceedings from the Policing Research Institute Meetings.* (pp. 151–168). National Institute of Justice and the Office of Community Oriented Policing Services.

Moore, M. H., Thacher, D., Dodge, A., & Moore, T. (2002). *Recognizing value in policing: The challenge of measuring police performance*. Police Executive Research Forum. https://scholar.harvard.edu/files/markmoore/files/20141204162104072.pdf.

Morgan, S., Murphy, D., & Horwitz, B. (2017). Police reform through data-driven management. *Police Quarterly*, 20(3), 275–294. https://doi.org/10.1177/1098611117709785.

Morrison, A., Lauer, C., & Sainz, A. (2023). Tyre Nichols case revives calls for change in police culture. *Associated Press*, January 29. https://apnews.com/article/law-enforcement-los-angeles-george-floyd-memphis-religion-21d9b66a447798e66e4f84a6b7bc3146.

Muja, S. (C). (2014). Basic etiquettes for effective communication. *Slideshare, a Scribd Company*. April 7, www.slideshare.net/Annasyy/etiquettes-33232236.

Murphy, K., & Cherney, A. (2012). Understanding cooperation with police in a diverse society. *British Journal of Criminology*, 52, 181–201. https://doi.org/10.1093/BJC/AZR065.

Nadolny, T. L., Penzenstadler, N., & Barton, G. (2024). America tested 100,000 forgotten rape kits. But justice remains elusive. November 12. *USA TODAY.* www.usatoday.com/story/news/investigations/2024/09/19/doj-rape-kit-test ing-program-results/74589312007/.

Nagin, D. S., & Telep, C. W. (2017). Procedural justice and legal compliance. *Annual Review of Law and Social Science*, 13, 5–28.

National Academies of Sciences, Engineering, and Medicine. (2025). *Law Enforcement Use of Predictive Policing Approaches: Proceedings of a Workshop*. The National Academies Press. https://doi.org/10.17226/ 28036.

National Advisory Commission on Civil Disorders. (1968). *Report of the National Advisory Commission on Civil Disorders*. Bantam Book. www .eisenhowerfoundation.org/docs/kerner.pdf.

National Fraternal Order of Police. (2024). 378 Officers shot in the line of duty in 2023. *Press Release*. January 2. https://fop.net/2024/01/378-officers-shot-in-the-line-of-duty-in-2023/.

Nelson, J. (2000). *Police brutality*. W. W. Norton.

Neusteter, S. R., Mapolski, M., Khogali, M., & O'Toole, M. (2019). *The 911 call processing system: A review of the literature as it relates to policing*. Vera Institute of Justice.

Nix, J., Huff, J., Wolfe, S. E., Pyrooz, D. C., & Mourtgos, S. M. (2024). When police pull back: Neighborhood-level effects of de-policing on violent and property crime, a research note. *Criminology*, 62(1), 156–171.

Oettmeier, T. N., & Wycoff, M. A. (1997). *Personnel performance evaluations in the community policing context*. Community Policing Forum. www.police forum.org/assets/docs/Free_Online_Documents/Community_Policing/per sonnel%20performance%20evaluations%20in%20the%20community% 20policing%20context.pdf.

Orth, U., Krauss, S., & Back, M.D. (2024). Development of narcissism across the life span: A meta-analytic review of longitudinal studies. *Psychological Bulletin*, 150(6), 643–665. https://doi.org/10.1037/bul0000436.

Ossei-Owusu, S. (2016). Race and the tragedy of quota-based policing. *The American Prospect*. November 3. https://prospect.org/justice/race-tragedy-quota-based-policing/.

Ostermann, M., Link, N. W., & Hyatt, J. M. (2024). Reframing the debate on legal financial obligations and crime: How accruing monetary sanctions impacts recidivism. *Criminology*, 62(2), 331–363.

Owens, E. G., Weisburd, D., Alpert, G., & Amendola, K. L. (2015). *Promoting Officer Integrity through Early Engagements and Procedural Justice in the Seattle Police Department: Final Report*. Grant No. 2012-IJ-CX-0009, awarded by the National Institute of Justice, Office of Justice Programs, U.S. Department of Justice. NCJ 249881.

Perry, G., Jonathan-Zamir, T., & Willis, J. J. (2023). The potential contribution of subjective causality to policing research: The case of the relationship between procedural justice and police legitimacy. In D. Weisburd, T. Jonathan-Zamir, G. Perry, & B. Hasisi (Eds.), *The future of evidence-based policing*. (2nd Ed., pp. 170–190). Cambridge University Press.

Petersen, K., Weisburd, D., Fay, S., Eggins, E., & Mazerolle, L. (2023). Police stops to reduce crime: A systematic review and meta-analysis. *Campbell Systematic Reviews*, 19(1), e1302.

Petrides, K. V., Mikolajczak, M., Mavroveli, S. et al. (2016). Developments in trait emotional intelligence research. *Emotion Review*, 8(4), 335–341. https://doi.org/10.1177/1754073916650493.

Pew Research Center. (2017). *Behind the badge: Amid protests and calls for reform, how police view their jobs, key issues and recent fatal encounters between Blacks and police*. Pew Research Center, January 11. www.pewsocialtrends.org/2017/01/11/behindthe-badge/.

Pickett, J. T., Graham, A., Nix, J., & Cullen, F. T. (2024). Officer diversity may reduce Black Americans' fear of police. *Criminology*, 62(1), 35–63.

Pierson, E., Simoiu, C., Overgoor, J. et al. (2020). A large-scale analysis of racial disparities in police stops across the United States. *Nature Human Behaviour*, 4(July), 736–745. https://5harad.com/papers/100M-stops.pdf.

Pincus, D. J. (1986). Communication satisfaction, job satisfaction, and job performance. *Human Communication Journal*, 12(3), 395–419. https://doi.org/10.1111/j.1468-2958.1986.tb00084.x.

Police Executive Research Forum. (2009). *Leadership matters: Police chiefs talk about their careers*. Police Executive Research Forum. ISBN: 978-1-934485-09-5.

Polis Solutions Inc. (2024). GE licenses key computer vision patents to Polis solutions: Technology supports expanded AI analysis of police body-worn camera video. January 30. *Polis Solutions*. www.police1.com/police-products/police-technology/software/video-analysis/ge-licenses-key-computer-vision-patents-to-polis-solutions.

President's Task Force on 21st Century Policing. (2015). *Final report of the President's Task Force on 21st Century Policing*. Office of Community Oriented Policing Services, U.S. Department of Justice. NCJ 248928.

Purnell, D. (2021). *Becoming abolitionists: Police, protests, and the pursuit of freedom*. Astra House.

Quattlebaum, M., Meares, T., & Tyler, T. (2018). *Principles of procedurally just policing*. The Justice Collaboratory at Yale Law School. https://law.yale.edu/

sites/default/files/principles_of_procedurally_just_policing_report_11.18.19.pdf.

Rahr, S., & Rice, S. K. (April, 2015). From warriors to guardians: Recommitting American police culture to democratic ideals. *New Perspectives in Policing*, Harvard Kennedy School Program in Criminal Justice Policy and Management. NCJ 48654.

Ratcliffe, J. H., Braga, A. A., Nagin, D. S., Webster, D. W., & Weisburd, D. (2024). When is a benefit a harm? The paradox of stop, question, and frisk. *Translational Criminology*, Fall Issue. George Mason University. https://cebcp.org/wp-content/uploads/2024/10/TC24-Fall2024.pdf.

Ravani, S. (2022). Oakland police department moves closer to end of federal oversight after nearly two decades under watch. *San Francisco Chronicle*, February 23. www.sfchronicle.com/eastbay/article/Oakland-police-department-moves-closer-to-end-of-16942061.php.

Reaves, B. A. (2016). *State and Local Law Enforcement Training Academies, 2013*. Bureau of Justice Statistics, Office of Justice Programs, US Department of Justice. July, 2016. NCJ 249784.

Reichel, P. L. (2022). Southern slave patrols as a transitional police type in the 19th century. *Brewminate*, September 9. https://brewminate.com/southern-slave-patrols-as-a-transitional-police-type-in-the-19th-century/.

Reisig, M. D. (1999). *Measuring performance in the era of community policing*. Executive Summary Series. Regional Community Policing Institute, East Lansing, MI.

Reiss, A. J., Jr. (1971). *The police and the public*. Yale University Press.

Remsberg, C. (1995). *Tactics for criminal patrol: Vehicle stops, drug discovery, and officer survival*. Calibre Press.

Richardson, L. S., & Goff, P. (2014). Interrogating racial violence. *Ohio State Journal of Criminal Law*, 12 (Fall). UC Irvine School of Law Research Paper No. 2015-13, 115-152. https://ssrn.com/abstract=2554003.

Roman, I. (2020). Women in policing: The numbers fall far short of the need. *Police Chief Online*, April 22. www.policechiefmagazine.org/women-in-policing/?ref=2ba34725db69fe5166d56ae855399c09.

Rosenbaum, D. P. (1986, Ed.) *Community crime prevention: Does it work?* Sage.

Rosenbaum, D. P. (1988). Community crime prevention: A review and synthesis of the literature. *Justice Quarterly*, 5, 323–395. https://doi.org/10.1080/07418828800089781.

Rosenbaum, D. P. (1993). Civil liberties and aggressive enforcement: Balancing the rights of individuals and society in the drug war. In R. C. Davis,

A. J. Lurigio, & D. P. Rosenbaum (Eds.), *Drugs and the Community*. (pp. 55–82). Charles C. Thomas.

Rosenbaum, D. P. (1994, Ed.). *The challenge of community policing: Testing the promises*. Sage.

Rosenbaum, D. P. (2002). Evaluating multi-agency anti-crime partnerships: Theory, design and measurement Issues. *Crime Prevention Studies*, 14, 171–225. https://popcenter.asu.edu/sites/default/files/library/crimepreven tion/volume_14/06-Rosenbaum.pdf.

Rosenbaum, D. P. (2004). Community policing and web-based communication: Addressing the new information imperative. In L. Fridell & M. A. Wycoff (Eds.), *Community policing: The past, present and future*. (pp. 93–114). Police Executive Research Forum. www.policeforum.org/assets/docs/ Free_Online_Documents/Community_Policing/community%20policing% 20-%20the%20past%20present%20and%20future%202004.pdf.

Rosenbaum, D. P. (2007). Police innovation post 1980: Assessing effectiveness and equity concerns in the information technology era. *Institute for the Prevention of Crime Review*, 1, 11–44. www.publicsafety.gc.ca/lbrr/arch ives/cnmcs-plcng/ripcr-v1-11-44-eng.pdf.

Rosenbaum, D. P. (2019). The limits of hot spots policing. In D. Weisburd & A. A. Braga (Eds.), *Police innovation: Contrasting perspectives*. (2nd Ed., pp. 314–344). Cambridge University Press.

Rosenbaum, D. P. (2024). Can we fix the "crisis of legitimacy" in American policing? Introducing performance metrics that matter to the community. Ideas in American Policing series, *National Policing Institute*. www.policinginstitute .org/publication/can-we-fix-the-crisis-of-legitimacy-in-american-policing/.

Rosenbaum, D. P., & Lavrakas, P. J. (1995). Self-reports about place: The application of survey and interview methods to the study of small areas. *Crime Prevention Studies*, 4, 285–314.

Rosenbaum, D. P., & Lawrence, D. S. (2017). Teaching procedural justice and communication skills during police–community encounters: Results of a randomized control trial with police recruits. *Journal of Experimental Criminology*, 13(3), 293–319. https://doi.org/10.1007/s11292-017-9293-3.

Rosenbaum, D. P., Lawrence, D. S., Hartnett, S. M., McDevitt, J., & Posick, C. (2015). Measuring procedural justice and legitimacy at the local level: The Police–Community Interaction Survey. *Journal of Experimental Criminology*, 11(3), 335–366.

Rosenbaum, D. P., Lurigio, A. J., & Davis, R. C. (1998). *The prevention of crime: Social and situational strategies*. Wadsworth.

Rosenbaum, D. P., Maskaly, J., Lawrence, D. S. et al. (2017). The police–community interaction survey: Measuring police performance in new ways.

Policing: An International Journal of Police Strategies & Management, 40(1), 112–127. https://doi.org/0.1108/PIJPSM-07-2016-0119.

Rosenbaum, D. P., & McCarty, W. P. (2017). Organizational justice and officer "buy in" in American policing. *Policing: An International Journal of Police Strategies & Management*, 40(1), 11–25. https://doi.org/0.1108/PIJPSM-07-2016-0114.

Rosenbaum, D. P., Schuck, A. M., Costello, S. K., Hawkins, D. F., & Ring, M. K. (2005). Attitudes toward the police: The effects of direct and vicarious experience. *Police Quarterly*, 8, 343–365. https://doi.org/10.1177/1098611104271085.

Roter, D. L., Larson, S., Shinitzky, H. et al. (2004). Use of an innovative video feedback technique to enhance communication skills training. *Medical Education*, 38, 145–157. https://doi.org/10.1111/j.1365-2923.2004.01754.x.

Rubinstein, J. (1973). *City police*. Farrar, Straus and Giroux.

Russek, Z., & Fitzpatrick, D. (2021). Early intervention systems. University of Chicago Crime Lab. https://urbanlabs.uchicago.edu/attachments/32d00780dcf1082f6b49c678f2afa838c9105f0c/store/b551dd26e caa556d96398cc4b4d2ca48ce57165a1c8187b5fc0d0a2f87b0/EIS.pdf.

Ryan, P., Luz, S., Albert, P. et al. (2019). Using artificial intelligence to assess clinicians' communication skills. *The British Medical Journal* (Online, January). https://doi.org/10.1136/bmj.l161.

Sahin, N., Braga, A., Apel, R., & Brunson, R. (2017). The impact of procedurally-just policing on citizen perceptions of police during traffic stops: The Adana Randomized Controlled Trial. *Journal of Quantitative Criminology*, 33, 701–726. https://doi.org/10.1007/S10940-016-9308-7.

Sampson, R. J., & Neil, R. (2024). The social foundations of racial inequalities in arrest over the life course and in changing times. *Criminology*, 62(2), 177–204.

Sampson, R. J., Raudenbush, S. W., & Earls, F. (1997). Neighborhoods and violent crime: A multilevel study of collective efficacy. *Science*, 277(5328), 918–924. https://doi.org/10.1126/science.277.5328.918.Google Scholar.

Schuck, A. M., & Rabe-Hemp, C. E. (2021). A longitudinal study of the effects of academy socialization on police integrity. *Police Quarterly*, 24(4), 578–606. https://doi.org/10.1177/109861112211029958.

Schuck, A. M., & Rosenbaum, D. P. (2006). Promoting safe and healthy neighborhoods: What research tells us about intervention. In K. Fulbright-Anderson (Ed.), *Community change: Theories, practices and evidence*, (pp. 61–140). The Aspen Institute.

Schunk, D. H., & Zimmerman, B. J. (1994, Eds.). *Self-regulation of learning and performance*. Erlbaum.

Scrivner, E. M. (1994). *The role of police psychology in controlling excessive force*. Report presented to the National Institute of Justice, U.S. Department of Justice. NCJ 146206. www.ojp.gov/pdffiles1/Digitization/146206NCJRS.pdf.

Seewer, J., & Dunklin, R. (2024). Policing group says officers must change how and when they use physical force on US streets. *Associated Press*. September 24. https://apnews.com/article/lethal-restraint-police-reform-law-enforcement-medics-3f746bc23ebc24c7c92d0f2468f13a29.

Seron, C., Periera, J., & Kovath, J. (2006). How citizens assess just punishment for police misconduct. *Criminology*, 44(4), 925–960.

Shah, S., Burch, J., & Neusteter, S. R. (2018, Eds). *Leveraging CompStat to include community measures in police performance management.* Perspectives from the Field. Vera Institute of Justice.

Sherman, L. W. (2013). The rise of evidence-based policing: Targeting, testing and tracking. In M. Tonry (Ed.), *Crime and justice: A review of research*. Vol. 42 (pp. 377–451). University of Chicago Press.

Sherman, L. W. (2023). Precision yes, pessimism no: A commentary on the Weisburd, Petersen & Fay (2023) Campbell Systematic Review. *Policing: A Journal of Policy and Practice*, 17, paad001. https://doi.org/10.1093/police/paad001.

Sherman, L. W., & Weisburd, D. (1995). General deterrent effects of police patrol in crime "hot spots": A randomized controlled trial. *Justice Quarterly*, 12, 626–648. https://doi.org/10.1080/07418829500096221.

Sia, D. (2023). Enhancing communication etiquette for effective interactions in business. *Linkedin*, June 1. www.linkedin.com/pulse/enhancing-communication-etiquette-effective-interactions-deepak-sai/.

Sinclair, S., Raffin-Bouchal, S., Venturato, L., Mijovic-Kondejewski, J., & Smith-MacDonald, L. (2017). Compassion fatigue: A meta-narrative review of the healthcare literature. *International Journal of Nursing Studies*, 69, 9–24. https://doi.org/10.1016/j.ijnurstu.2017.01.003.

Sipe, J. W., & Frick, D. M. (2009). *Seven pillars of servant leadership*. Paulist Press.

Shon, P. (2024). 'I clocked you going 50 in a 25': Discourse-based critique of police procedural justice research through a sequential exploration of 'voice' and excuses in traffic encounters. *The British Journal of Criminology*, 2023, XX, 1–19. https://doi.org/10.1093/bjc/azad015.

Skolnick, J. H. (1975). *Justice without trial: Law enforcement in democratic society*. (2nd Ed.). John Wiley & Sons.

Skogan, W. G. (2003, Ed.). *Community policing: Can it work?* Wadsworth.

Skogan, W. G. (2023). *Stop and frisk and the politics of crime in Chicago*. Oxford University Press.

Skogan, W., & Frydl, K. (2004, Eds). *Fairness and effectiveness in policing: The evidence*. National Research Council Committee to Review Research on Police Policy and Practices. The National Academies Press.

Skogan, W. G., & Hartnett, S. M. (1997). *Community policing, Chicago style*. Oxford University Press.

Skolnick, J. H., & Fyfe, J. J. (1993). *Above the law: Police and the excessive use of force*. Free Press.

Southall, A. (2022). "Negligent and sexist": Why rape survivors asked Feds to investigate N.Y.P.D. *New York Times*. July 28. www.nytimes.com/2022/07/28/nyregion/nypd-doj-special-victims-investigation.html.

Sparrow, M. K. (2015). Measuring performance in a modern police organization. *New Perspectives in Policing Bulletin*. U.S. Department of Justice, *National Institute of Justice*, NCJ 248476.

Spence, G. (2015). *Police state: How America's cops get away with murder*. St. Martin's Press.

Stanton, C. (2022). Police, firefighters die by suicide more often than in line of duty. Why rates remain high. *USA Today*. June 10. www.usatoday.com/story/news/nation/2022/06/10/high-suicide-rate-police-firefighters-mental-health/7470846001/.

Starzynski, L. S., Ullman, S. E., Filipas, H. H., & Townsend, S. M. (2005). Correlates of women's sexual assault disclosure to informal and formal support sources. *Violence and Victims*, 20, 417–432.

Stecklow, S. (2024). New proposed rules would lower the bar for stripping police officers of their badges in Illinois. *IPM New*. October 11. Invisible Institute. https://ipmnewsroom.org/new-proposed-rules-would-lower-the-bar-for-stripping-police-officers-of-their-badges-in-illinois/.

Stepler, R. (2017). Female police officers' on-the-job experiences diverge from those of male officers. January 17. Pew Research Center. www.pewresearch.org/short-reads/2017/01/17/female-police-officers-on-the-job-experiences-diverge-from-those-of-male-officers/.

Stewart, C. L., & Cash, W. B. Jr. (2008). *Interviewing: Principles and practices*. (12th Ed.). McGraw-Hill.

Stone, D., Patton, B., & Henn, S. (2023). *Difficult conversations: How to discuss what matters most*. Penguin Books.

Suddler, C. (2019). *Presumed criminal: Black youth and the justice system in Postward, New York*. New York University Press.

Tajfel, H., & Turner, J. C. (1979). An integrative theory of intergroup conflict. In In W. G. Austin, & S. Worchel (Eds.), *The social psychology of intergroup relations*. (pp. 33–37). Monterey, CA: Brooks/Cole.

Tankebe, J. (2013). Viewing things differently: The dimensions of public perceptions of police legitimacy. *Criminology: An Interdisciplinary Journal*, 51(1), 103–135. https://doi.org/10.1111/j.1745-9125.2012.00291.x.

Tapp, S. N., & Davis, E. J. (2022). *Contacts between police and the public, 2020.* U.S. Department of Justice, Bureau of Justice Statistics. Special Report, November. NCJ 304527. https://bjs.ojp.gov/library/publications/con tacts-between-police-and-public-2020.

Terrill, W., & Reisig, M. D. (2003). Neighborhood context and police use of force. *Journal of Research in Crime and Delinquency*, 40(3), 291–321. https://doi.org/10.1177/0022427803253800.

The Decision Lab. (2024). Reactance theory. Downloaded March 10, 2024. https://thedecisionlab.com/reference-guide/psychology/reactance-theory.

Tiratelli, M., Quinton, P., & Bradford, B. (2018). Does stop and search deter crime? Evidence from ten years of London-wide data. *British Journal of Criminology*, 58, 1212–1231. Advance Access publication 27. https://type set.io/pdf/does-stop-and-search-deter-crime-evidence-from-ten-years-of-1avs0alnqq.pdf.

Todd, A. R., Bodenhausen, G. V., Richeson, J. A., & Galinsky, A. D. (2011). Perspective taking combats automatic expressions of racial bias. *Journal of Personality and Social Psychology*, 100(6), 1027–1042. https://doi.org/10.1037/a0022308(opens in a new window/tab).

Toews, R. (2023). Transformers revolutionized AI. What will replace them? *Forbes*, September 3. www.forbes.com/sites/robtoews/2023/09/03/trans formers-revolutionized-ai-what-will-replace-them/.

Tully, T. (2024). For 8 Months, traffic enforcement on New Jersey's highways plummeted. *New York Times*, December 8. www.nytimes.com/2024/12/08/nyregion/new-jersey-state-police-slowdown.html.

Twenge, J. M. (2023). *The real differences between Gen Z, Millennials, Gen X, Boomers, and Silents – and what they mean for America's future.* Atria Books.

Tyler, T. R. (1990). *Why people obey the law.* Yale University Press.

Tyler, T. R. (2004). Enhancing police legitimacy. *The Annals of the American Academy of Political and Social Science*, 593(1), 84–99. https://doi.org/10.1177/0002716203262627.

Tyler, T. R. (2005). Policing in black and white: Ethnic group differences in trust and confidence in the police. *Police Quarterly*, 8(3), 322–342. https://doi.org/10.1177/1098611104271105.

Tyler, T. R. (2006). *Why people obey the law.* Princeton University Press.

Tyler, T. R. (2014). What are legitimacy and procedural justice in policing? And why are they becoming key elements of police leadership? In C. Fischer

(Ed.), *Legitimacy and procedural justice: A new element of police leadership.* (pp. 6–35). Police Executive Research Forum.

Tyler, T. R. & Fagan, J. A. (2006). Legitimacy and cooperation: Why do people help the police fight crime in their communities? *Ohio State Journal of Criminal Law*, 6, 231–275.

Tyler, T. R., & Huo, Y. (2002). *Trust in the law: Encouraging public cooperation with the police and courts*. Russell Sage Foundation. Google Scholar.

Tyler, T. R., & Jackson, J. (2013). Popular legitimacy and the exercise of legal authority: Motivating compliance, cooperation and engagement. *Psychology Public Policy and Law*. November. doi: 10.1037/a0034514. www.research gate.net/publication/249643866_Popular_Legitimacy_and_the_Exercise_of_ Legal_Authority_Motivating_Compliance_Cooperation_and_Engagement.

Tyler, T. R., & Meares, T. (2021). Revisiting broken windows: The role of the community and the police in promoting community engagement. *NYU Annual Survey of American Law*, 76, 637–656. Google Scholar.

Tyler, T., & Nobo, C. (2022). *Legitimacy-based policing and the promotion of community vitality*. Cambridge University Press. https://doi.org/10.1017/ 9781009308014.

U.S. Department of Justice. (2017). *The Civil Rights Division's pattern and practice police reform work: 1994–Present*. Civil Rights Division, U.S. Department of Justice. www.justice.gov/crt/file/922421/dl.

U.S. Department of Justice. (2024). *Officer safety and wellness resources*. Office of Associate Attorney General, U.S. Department of Justice. www .justice.gov/asg/officer-safety-and-wellness-resources.

Ullman, S. E. (1999). Social support and recovery from sexual assault: A review. *Aggression and Violent Behavior: A Review Journal*, 4, 343–358.

Ullman, S. E. (2000). Psychometric characteristics of the social reactions questionnaire. *Psychology of Women Quarterly*, 24, 257–271.

Van Maanen, J. (1983). The boss: First-line supervision in an American police agency. In M. Punch (Ed.), *Control in the police organization*. (pp. 275–317). MIT Press.

VanSickle, A. (2024). The town at the center of a Supreme Court battle over homelessness. *New York Times*. April 20. www.nytimes.com/2024/04/20/us/ supreme-court-homelessness-oregon.html?searchResultPosition=3.

Vasu, M. L., Stewart, D. W., & Garson, G. D. (1998). *Organizational behavior and public management*. (3rd Ed.). Marcel Dekker.

Voigt, R., Camp, N. P., Prabhakaran, V., & Eberhardt, J. L. (2017). Language from police body camera footage shows racial disparities in officer respect. June 5. *Proceedings of the National Academy of Sciences*, 114(25), 6521–6526. www.pnas.org/cgi/doi/10.1073/pnas.1702413114.

Waeraas, A. (2009). On Weber: Legitimacy and legitimation in public relations. In O. Ihlen & M. Fredriksson (Eds.), *Public relations and social theory: Key figures, concepts, and developments.* (pp. 301–322). Routledge.

Walker, S. (1977). *A critical history of police reform: The perils of professionalism.* Lexington Books.

Walker, S. (2017). *Twenty years of DOJ "pattern or practice" investigations of local police: Achievements, limitations, and questions.* University of Nebraska at Omaha.

Walker, S., Alpert, G. P., & Kenney, D. J. (2000). Early warning systems for police: Concepts, history, and issues. *Police Quarterly,* 3(2), 132–152.

Walker, S., & Archbold, C. A. (2020). *The new world of police accountability.* 3rd Ed. Sage.

Walker, S., & Milligan, S. O. (2006). *Strategies for intervening with officers through early intervention systems: A guide for front-line supervisors.* Police Executive Research Forum. ISBN: 1-878734-93-8.

Walsh, W. (2001). CompStat: An analysis of an emerging police paradigm. *Policing: An International Journal of Police Management and Strategies,* 24, 347–362.

Walters, G. D., & Bolger, P. C. (2018). Procedural justice perceptions, legitimacy beliefs, and compliance with the law: A meta-analysis. *Journal of Experimental Criminology,* 15(3), 341–372. https://doi.org/10.1007/s11292-018-9338-2.Google Scholar.

Washington Post. (2024). Fatal force: 1,141 people have been shot and killed by police in the past 12 months. *The Washington Post Fatal Force Database.* February 7. www.washingtonpost.com/pr/2022/12/06/pulitzer-prize-winning-fatal-force-database-updated-with-federal-ids-police-departments-involved-fatal-shootings/.

Watson, A. C., Compton, M. T., & Pope, L. G. (2019). *Crisis response services for people with mental illnesses or intellectual and developmental disabilities: A review of the literature on police-based and other first response models.* VERA Institute of Justice. Google Scholar.

Weisburd, D. W., & Braga, A. A. (2006, Eds.). *Prospects and problems in an era of policing innovation: Contrasting perspectives.* Cambridge University Press.

Weisburd, D. W., & Braga, A. A. (2019). Hot spots policing as a model for police innovation. In D. Weisburd & A. A. Braga (Eds.), *Police innovation: Contrasting perspectives.* 2nd Ed. (pp. 291–313). Cambridge University Press.

Weisburd, D. W., & Eck, J. E. (2017, Eds.). *Unraveling the crime-place connection: New directions in theory and policy.* (Volume 22 of *Advances in Criminological Theory*). Routledge.

Weisburd, D., & Majmundar, M. K. (2018, Eds.). *Proactive policing: Effects on crime and communities*. Committee on proactive policing: Effects on crime, communities, and civil liberties. The National Academies Press. https://nap .nationalacademies.org/catalog/24928/proactive-policing-effects-on-crime- and-communities.

Weisburd, D., Petersen, K., & Fay, S. A. (2023). Does scientific evidence support the widespread use of SQFs as a proactive policing strategy? *Policing: A Journal of Policy and Practice*, 17, 1–17. Advanced online publication. https://doi.org/10.1093/police/paac098.

Weisburd, D., Petersen, K., & Fay, S. A. (2024). It is time for "Big Science" in SQF research: The questions are important enough and the potential harms of "Small Science" great enough. *Policing: A Journal of Policy and Practice*, 18, paae098. https://doi.org/10.1093/police/paae098.

Weisburd, D., Telep, C. W., Vovak, H. et al. (2022). Reforming the police through procedural justice training: A multicity randomized trial at crime hot spots. *PSNA*, 119 (14), e2118780119. https://doi.org/10.1073/pnas.2118780119.

Weiss, A., & Rosenbaum, D. P. (2009). *Illinois traffic stop statistics study, 2008 Annual Report*. Illinois Department of Transportation.

Weitzer, R. (2000). White, Black, or blue cops? Race and citizen assessments of police officers. *Journal of Criminal Justice*, 28(4), 313–324. https://doi.org/ 10.1016/S0047-2352(00)00043-X.

Weitzer, R. & Tuch, S.A. (2005). Determinants of public satisfaction with the police. *Police Quarterly*, 8(3), 279–297. https://doi.org/10.1177/ 1098611104271106.

Wheller, L., Quinton, P., Fildes, A., & Mills, A. (2013). *The greater Manchester police procedural justice training experiment*. College of Policing, Coventry. https://library.college.police.uk/docs/college-of-policing/Technical-Report.pdf.

White, M. D. (2007). *Current issues and controversies in policing*. Pearson Education.

White, M. D. (2014). *Police officer body-worn cameras: Assessing the evidence*. Office of Community Oriented Policing Services, U.S. Department of Justice. NCJ 247941.

White, M. D., & Fradella, H. F. (2016). *Stop-and-Frisk: The use and abuse of a controversial police tactic*. New York University Press.

White, M. D., Saladeen, M., & Martin, A. (2023). Working with BWC Metadata. Webinar, October 19. Body-Worn Camera Training and Technical Assistance Program. https://bwctta.com/tta/webinars/working- bwc-metadata.

Wilkerson, I. (2011). *The warmth of other suns*. Vintage Books.

Williams, K. (2015). *Our enemies in blue: Police and power in America*. AK Press.

Willis, J. J., Mastrofski, S. D., & Kochel, T. R. (2010). The co-implementation of CompStat and community policing. *Journal of Criminal Justice*, 38(5), 969–980. www.sciencedirect.com/science/article/pii/S0047235210001479.

Wood, G., Tyler, T. R., & Papachristos, A. V. (2020). Procedural justice training reduces police use of force and complaints against officers. *Proceeding of the National Academy of Sciences*, 117(18), 9815–9821. https://doi.org/10.1073/pnas.1920671117.

Woolington, R., & Lewis, M. (2018). Portland homeless accounted for majority of police arrests in 2017, analysis finds. *The Oregonian/Oregonlive*, June 27. www.oregonlive.com/portland/2018/06/portland_homeless_accounted_fo.html.

Worden, R. E., Harris, C., & McLean, S. J. (2014). Risk assessment and risk management in policing. *Policing: An International Journal of Police Strategies & Management*, 37(2), 239–258. https://doi.org/10.1108/PIJPSM-12-2012-0088.

Worden, R. E., & Shepard, R. L. (1996). Demeanor, crime and police behavior: A reexamination of the Police Services Study data. *Criminology*, 34(1), 83–105.

Xiao, W., Lin, X., Li, X. et al. (2021). The influence of emotion and empathy on decisions to help others. *Sage Open*, 11(2). https://journals.sagepub.com/doi/epub/10.1177/21582440211014513.

Yale Law School Justice Collaboratory. (2023). *Principles of procedurally just policing*. https://law.yale.edu/sites/default/files/principles_of_procedurally_just_policing_report_11.18.19.pdf.

Yancey-Bragg, N. (2023). Police misconduct settlements can cost millions, but departments rarely feel the impact. *USA Today*, November 17. www.usatoday.com/story/news/nation/2023/11/17/who-pays-police-misconduct-settlements/71516795007/.

Zaki, J. (2017). We're experiencing an empathy shortage, but we can fix it together. *TEDx Talk*, September. www.ted.com/talks/jamil_zaki_we_re_experiencing_an_empathy_shortage_but_we_can_fix_it_together?subtitle=en.

Printed by Integrated Books International,
United States of America